NG:She
women leading the conversation

Survivors Speaking
for a Change

edited by Ros Forsey and Jo Welch
from NG:She

with a foreword by Karen Ingala Smith

published by Big White Shed, Nottingham, England
ISBN 978-1-9164035-1-2
Printed and bound in EU by Booksfactory
Cover: Emily Catherine Illustration

We dedicate this book to all of our sister survivors and victims everywhere, because we believe that stories and sisterhood are powerful and because we want you to know that there can be a better day.

CONTENTS

INTRODUCTION

The women featured in this book, and those who have worked on it behind the scenes, in many different ways, are all domestic violence and abuse survivors. We came together as a result of a Domestic Violence Awareness and Helping Skills training programme run by NG:She Community Interest Company between 2016 and 2018 across Nottinghamshire. The stories and poems published here are transcribed from a series of podcasts which are available on-line via NG:She's Facebook page.

We are women aged from 17 to 63. We are disabled and able-bodied, Black, Muslim, white and mixed race, lesbian, bisexual and heterosexual, working class and middle class. We are poets, activists, mothers, teachers, apprentices, support workers, call centre operatives, librarians, dog lovers, campaigners, students, audio producers and domestic violence advocates.

The stories we share here and in our accompanying podcasts are not only of our experiences of violence and abuse, but of the highs and lows of our survival. We wanted, in addition to sharing our painful memories, to talk of our lives as they are today, and although these are still, and will always be, touched by what has happened to us, they are not determined by it and on our best days we can know love, happiness and peace.

We wanted to share these stories and poems to enable women who are currently experiencing domestic violence and abuse, or newly escaped from it, to believe that horror can eventually pass, that anger is ok and that even we, the survivors of the epidemic of male violence that is currently sweeping the world, can know joy and laughter. We want all sister victims and survivors everywhere to know that even in our most painful and lonely moments, there can be a better day.

We are Lisa, Mimi, Dee, Irene, Ameena, Rosie, Michaela, Tracey, CSS, Jane, Jo and Ros and we are survivors speaking for a change.

We dedicate this book to all of our sister survivors and victims everywhere because we believe that stories and sisterhood are powerful.

If you or someone close to you is experiencing domestic violence or abuse, then please see the helpline and support information at the back of this book.

FOREWORD

In the latest full year for which there are records, over 1.1 million 'domestic abuse related incidents' were reported to the police in England and Wales which means that approximately one-third of all violent crimes reported to the police relate to domestic violence and abuse. But in most cases, domestic violence and abuse is not reported to the police, some women may tell only a close friend or family member, some women will live their life with abuse and tell no-one.

The first refuge in the UK was opened in West London in 1971, now there are over 500 in England, Wales, Scotland and Northern Ireland, with community-based support available in many towns and cities. The government currently provides hundreds of thousands of pounds to support services for women subjected to domestic violence and abuse in a way that might have seemed inconceivable, miraculous even, to the women developing those first refuges and community services in the 1970s, but this has come at the cost of independence. In effect, most services developed by women for women are now 'owned' by local authorities through contracts. Local authorities decide what is in women's best interests and who is best placed to provide it and too often they have decided that low cost is more important than small independent woman-led, woman-centred specialist organisations supporting women. More recently, austerity measures have brought another assault on specialist women's services, domestic and sexual violence services aren't statutory, which means that councils are not required to provide services for women who have been subjected to men's violence, they can simply choose not to and last year in Sunderland, the council decided that it would no longer fund a single refuge. Women-led specialist services for women by women are under threat but when asked, women survivors of abuse tell us that they prefer, feel safer, better supported and better understood when they are supported by women in women-only spaces.

So many times I have heard well-intentioned people say that domestic violence is 'gender-neutral' or doesn't discriminate by sex, race, religion, age, or disability and there's always someone ready to ask the question "What about the men?' Whilst it's true that domestic violence crosses boundaries of class, race, age, and religion - and can affect men - there are some differences in abuse between these groups, differences in how easy it is to access support, differences in whether we are believed or judged, and differences in how we are understood. Across all these differences one thing is constant: that domestic violence and abuse does discriminate. Yes, men can be victims, but women are overwhelmingly the victims and men are overwhelmingly the perpetrators. Domestic violence is a form of men's violence against women, it doesn't just discriminate against women, it is a form of discrimination against women and it is linked to inequality between the sexes. That's why when we think about how we could end domestic violence, we have to think big; it goes beyond, but of course includes, how people behave in their relationships and even beyond laws around violence and sex equality. To end domestic violence we have to look at how and why women and men are kept unequal, even when the law says that's wrong. We have to change everyday attitudes towards women and men and our different expectations of women and men and understand how these ideas prop up violence and inequality.

Men's violence against women is all too often deadly and one of the starkest ways sex differences in domestic violence are illustrated is in the figures for domestic homicides. In the UK, over 70% of those killed by a current or former partner are women killed by men, of the men killed about two-thirds are killed by men and where they are killed by women, in many cases they are killed by a woman that they've been abusing for years; where men kill women this is rarely the case, mostly when men kill their female partners or exes, it is after years of abusing her.

In January 2012, after the murder of a young woman close to where I live in East London, I stated making a list of the names of women killed by men, quite simply because there seemed to be so many and I wanted to try to figure out how many women had been killed since the start of the year. It turned out that eight women had been killed by men in the first 3 days of January. It never felt right to stop, because that would feel too much like I'm saying that the next woman isn't worth counting and commemorating and I just don't want to have to say that. I've recorded the names of over 900 women who have been killed by men in the UK on my blog Counting Dead Women over the the past six and a half years, so a man has killed a woman every 2.6 days and about two-thirds of them are women who were killed by a partner or ex-partner.

But it's important to remember that although domestic violence or intimate partner homicides happen all too often, compared to the women who live with or who escape from a violent man, they are rare. For most women, a different future is possible, but reaching out, especially for the first time, can be hard. Who do you tell? Will they believe you? Will they judge you? What difference could it make? What about those of us who even blame ourselves?

The fight against domestic violence and abuse has been led by women, supporting women. We wouldn't have a network of refuges and domestic violence and abuse services or Rape Crisis centres if feminists, activists, and survivors (and of course many women are both) had not created them because we realised that we - women - needed them, and we - women - wanted to support other women facing what we have faced. And women have succeeded in creating change. The largest ever study of government responses to violence against women and girls looked at 70 countries from 1975 to 2005 and they found that the most important factor influencing policy change was feminist activism. It played a more critical role than left-wing governments, the numbers of women in power and national wealth. Women, feminists, are those who make change for women facing men's violence. This book joins that proud history of women supporting women. Women remembering those days before they told anyone, before they could see a way out or a future in which they felt safe, secure and happy and have reached out to others who may be in a similar position to offer hope. It is written for women in violent and abusive relationships by the most important experts, those who have been there themselves. Women creating change for women, one woman at a time.

by Karen Ingala Smith

Karen Ingala Smith is co-creator with Women's Aid of *The Femicide Census,* a groundbreaking project enabling the monitoring and analysis of men's fatal violence against women, with the aim of contributing to the reduction of the number of women killed by men. She is also CEO of nia - a London-based domestic and sexual violence charity working to end men's violence against women and girls. Karen is also a survivor of domestic violence and abuse in childhood. She grew up in a family where the man she thought was her father was violent to her mum and their children.

AMEENA
When he snapped, I snapped back

When I'm on the helpline and I've spoken to women, I can hear that relief in them. It just gives me a buzz and I absolutely love it. To know that I've made a difference in somebody's life. I've actually had feedback, where a woman was in a very, very horrible place and I spoke to her and just listened to her, and acknowledged her feelings, and I said, 'yes you were right - you don't deserve to be treated the way you were'. I received feedback a few weeks later from her that I had stopped her from harming herself, and honestly that was the best feeling ever.

No amount of money can give you that feeling, and I absolutely thrive on that.

I've always been drawn to help people that are, what society sees as 'damaged'. I'm also damaged from the domestic violence that I've suffered. But there is hope after that. I have more empathy, I'm able to help people, I'm drawn to people who've had it tough, and that's why, because of my personal experiences, I wanted to do this.

Ameena's Story

I've always been drawn to helping people from disadvantaged backgrounds - people who have suffered in some way. I want them to see the potential that they have, and to bring out the best in them. Domestic violence was something that was personal to me. My work started off with helping women from the BAME community empower themselves, go out there and access services which they were unable to do, but because I'm passionate about helping people with DV, I wanted to gain some experience of that so I could go into working in that field.

People weren't accessing health services. They weren't accessing the local facilities that were available - like local education opportunities. A lot of women weren't even aware of them. The services that were there weren't tailored to their needs. There were language barriers and there were cultural barriers. The Asian women that I was helping didn't want to go and use services where there were men, so I helped them by creating specific services that were just women only. This was about ten years ago, so we didn't have hardly anything like that then.

Initially, I took a career break. A ten year career break actually, and although I thought I was quite strong - I was educated, I was independent, I could drive, I had a fantastic job - when I left work to bring up my children, I found myself... a woman who used to help other women to become empowered... totally disempowered! I went into a cycle of just not going out and just concentrating on the children. I just gave up my everyday life. I didn't realise how easily that could happen. For 10 years I became completely de-skilled. I wanted to re-skill myself, and I started off by volunteering at a Women's Centre. I used to be on one of the helplines there, and I did that for about a year.

Then I became employed for three years. My employment wasn't related to support work or women's work or any empowerment… it was in a call centre. I absolutely loved it though. I met amazing people there, people I wouldn't normally meet in my everyday life, because I'd become so secluded at home and had no friends. I had no support network of my own, but I met these amazing people at work. They were from all different backgrounds. Different races, different religions, different sexual orientations, genders. I loved that diversity, and I embraced it. But I wasn't getting any job satisfaction from it. Although I loved the work and it gave me economic empowerment - and I became more independent in that sense - I still didn't have job satisfaction, so I started volunteering back on the helpline again, which I still loved.

I did actually apply for a position within the domestic violence field, and I didn't get it because I didn't have enough experience, so I let that go and I stopped trying for ages. But I thought I am going to kick myself later on if I don't go back and do this, so I came on NG:She's Domestic Violence Helping Skills training programme and I absolutely loved it. I started applying for more positions but I didn't get any interviews for the first few applications, then I got an interview and I got the job and it's the best thing ever.

I've seen my mum struggle with abuse all my life. I mean, as far back as I can remember actually, she was abused by my father. I remember occasions when… I think I was 8 years old and I came back from school one day, and my mum opened the door, and she was covered in blood. It's one of the most vivid pictures that I'll never forget. She was covered in blood from top to bottom. She was hospitalised so many times. Nobody came to help her though, for whatever reason and she was scared, because of the culture, because of what people would say - that she'd failed in her marriage, and so on and so forth.

But, although she was abused and beaten by him, she's always remained strong. She's always told us to go and follow our dreams, to become educated and be independent. So it's my mother that gave us that power. My empowerment comes from my Mum. She's an amazing woman. Another reason why I wanted to come back into this field of work is that last year she was diagnosed with cancer. She's known my passion for helping others and wanting to empower women, so although she knew I was happy where I worked, she knew it wasn't the best that I could be... and she was always asking me, 'have you got the job that you want'… and I was always saying, 'yes mum, I'll get round to it'… and then I realised, oh my gosh, life's too short, and that's part of the reason that I decided to go into doing this as well. So my inspiration, my power is my Mum.

No matter how damaged you are, there is always something you can give back, and you do heal. I mean I remember, I used to - I've recently found out - 'dissociate'... and I had no idea what it was I was going through.

I can't even remember how old I was, but I was very, very young. Maybe eight... and just before I would fall asleep, I'd go into a trance I couldn't come out of. It was a wave of time almost stopping. The first time it happened, I didn't know what it was, and in that moment I used to question, like, 'who am I?' And even though I was so young, I used to question 'where am I and what is this world around me ?' Everything was slow motion, and I couldn't bring myself out of it. I used to wait for it to come, and finish, and then I'd be able to breathe. Although my breathing was fine, it was just everything around me was really slow.

I've realised that I remember these moments vividly, as I have experienced this again more recently... and I only found out then that this could have been a result of the trauma. And I'm so thankful that it happened, because I've recently - during my studies - found out that it was my mind's way of coping with the situation at the time.

So, it was a culture of secrecy. The whole issue of not telling on your dad - because although what he did was abhorrent, we still loved him. Still do... and the experiences are part of me, and they are what makes me... and I've come to a point in my life where, although they were horrible and traumatic, I know I'm still an amazing person because of it. I'm able to, and I love helping people around me and I'm thinking, if I didn't have that experience, maybe I wouldn't be the way I am now?

Because I was the middle one - my oldest sister and brother weren't on the receiving end of it as much as I was, and it was always me and my mother that suffered the main outbursts. But I always, always had the urge to protect my younger sister. So much so that, although I know I'm safe right now, and in my everyday life I'm completely fine, I still sometimes have nightmares, that he's trying to get at my younger sister, and I wake up in cold sweats. I was always the one that was there to protect her, as a buffer, but no… we didn't speak to nobody.

At the age of 14, when he snapped, I snapped back. I stood up to him, and he was really violent. I don't think he realised that I was at the point where I'd had enough. There was a situation where he got help from other people in the family as well. So we were like in a physical brawl, and he was holding me and he was beating me.

We just walked out. I remember leaving the house, barefooted. It was my younger sister. My sister and my older brother weren't there. It was just me, my younger sister and my mum, and we just walked out, got into a taxi and drove off.

When I say drove off - we went to a property that a family member owned… and we stayed there.

I called and managed to get through to the police, because during this incident, my younger sister had also managed to get through to the police, but she wasn't able to talk to them. So the police did turn up, and they did find us, but other family members convinced me not to tell them the full story, so I wasn't able to get help. But we were left alone by my dad there. That was where the most amazing years of my life were - when it was just my mother and my younger sister and I.

That was just full of happiness, and we were just free. There had been so much control in everything, in every aspect of our life. It wasn't just physical abuse, it was that he just controlled everything. He had access to the phones, and he wouldn't allow us to use them - even my mother. She wasn't allowed to use the phone and she had no money. After we left we were able to get benefits for my mum, so she gained that independence.

I wouldn't allow him into the house. With all I'd experienced, I was very strong willed. So he'd knock on the door and I wouldn't allow my Mum to open the door. I was scared, because after that experience, that final incident - the most violent one, it was the most violent he'd ever been towards me, and it was horrible, because I was shaky. I'd constantly be on edge. I just wouldn't allow him in, and I said to my Mum, 'look if he comes in, I'm leaving you as well. It's not fair on me to be exposed to him.'

So we lived there until I was 16. My Mum was amazing.

We all flourished without him, we got into education, got brilliant GCSE's, did A Levels, went to university - my younger sister as well - she did really well.

At one point I was almost… because of my strength…. I was scared I was like him. Physically he's very strong as well, but, I think, yeah - I was almost scared I'd be like him. But, there's no way… no way on earth.

He used to have this famous line where he said, 'you've got two ears and one mouth'. He'd always shut me down with that line, and it was always me that he used to shut down as well. It was like we got too much 'be quiet, quiet'. He'd abruptly cut me off. I feel that's had an effect. I'm not very confident. I mean, once I'm comfortable with people, I'm ok, but when I meet new people, I am petrified. When somebody tells you to be quiet all the time, constantly, you just become a quiet person.

As a result of it I have become a feminist. I've got a daughter, who I just want to just smash through that glass ceiling ! Her teacher actually described her as bossy, and I gave her a high five and I was like, 'I'm so proud of you… you're not bossy, you are independent, you are amazing, there's no such thing as bossy'. You know, I tell her, 'you're equal to men, if not better'. I teach my sons to respect women too.

I'm hoping my experiences have taught me to become more demanding of life and to challenge discrimination of any sort, whether that be workplace or just generally in life. I just won't stand for it.

Every woman has a right to freedom, and to do whatever she pleases with that freedom and to be happy, just to be happy - every woman has that right.

A lot of women are made to feel that no… men's happiness should be put before theirs… and that's not true. I want women to know that they've got that strength, to stick up for that right… and I want that, I want all women, everybody to be equal.

My new job is general support for women 18 and over, who have suffered domestic violence. Organising sessions where women can come in and talk, and feel free, and fill in DASH checklists and things like that.

There is light at the end of the tunnel and it is worth that fight, because when you're in that situation, it feels like it's never going to end… and it's a fight that's not worth fighting, but it is worth it, honestly… and it doesn't last, the fight and the struggle, it doesn't last.

Once you're out of that situation, there is a way over it, and there is a way of becoming… of letting your true self out. I'm not saying you become a better person, because you are a better person, it's just that you're caged, and your light has been taken over by that darkness… but there is a way out of it, and your light will shine.

Just put up that fight, just take that first step. It's that first step that's the hardest to take. Just take that step, and honestly, get the right support, go to the right places. Sometimes you'll tell somebody, but they don't have the knowledge, and they'll give you the wrong advice, and they'll say… 'yeah he'll change,' or 'what will people say?' But those are the wrong people to go to. Women's Aid are amazing.

Just make that call, you don't have to tell them who you are and hopefully you'll find a way out.

IRENE
I'm a fighter and I will fight for justice.

Hey, I'm Irene and I come to Nottingham at 19 as a young girl, as a runaway from domestic abuse, in the family. I went to the train station as a youngster, and I went,
> *where am I going to go?*

...and I ended up saying Nottingham Central - and I'm here ever since.

Domestic violence actually started when I was a child. There was physical violence, as well as sexual violence in my family network. I escaped that. I came here as a survivor of childhood trauma and abuse, and I vowed that no man on this earth would ever put his hand on me again.

To peter thank you

Irene Khodt

Irene's Story

For the first 12 years in Nottingham it was pretty hard. I already had two small children when I arrived and I had another son during that time… and I came out and disclosed my childhood trauma, due to the fact that I was having problems with my oldest child. I eventually had to have a DNA test to see if it was my father's child. This is how deep my trauma went.

I'd come to realise there were many young people like myself in the system, who'd been let down and I thought, what can I do to help? So I started up a little cleaning company, giving single mums a job in the day time… just to help them manage better, teach them about finances. We used to go shopping together - budgeting - little things that mattered. People don't understand that these things do matter when you've got a family, you don't get a handbook to be a parent, we have to learn, and so we learned together.

I made a lot of mistakes, but I learned from my mistakes, and I used them to try to teach others. I just kept trying to battle on and keep surviving.

You don't actually realise it's 'control' at the time. You think it's love, and that they care about you. All these things, the nice things that happen in relationships, they make you forget about all the bad things. If it's too good to be true, it's usually too good to be true. There's usually a darker side, and 90% of people find these things out at the end of the relationship. We start to analyse it and reflect on things we didn't notice in the beginning. We don't do it until then because we are wrapped up in the moment, the 'love', or thinking 'they'll change', or thinking they're not really like 'that'. But actually, you know, even the nicest, sweetest person you come across can be the most evil, and they don't actually need to lift a finger.

This is the problem... that people think that domestic abuse is all about getting a smack or a punch. It's the mental, the emotional, the psychological abuse that does more damage than a punch though. A bruise heals… but that psychological and that emotional and mental abuse doesn't… and the damage it does to children is absolutely horrendous. People don't see that, and especially men don't see it.

What are we teaching our daughters? What are we teaching our sons? It's OK to treat a woman like that? It's OK for a woman to accept that? I don't think so. I am making it a point now in my voluntary work, to make sure young people know they don't have to be touched, they don't have to be spoken to in a bad manner. They're not being downgraded because they wear a short skirt… or they might be gothic or whatever… or a different gender.

Society's got to change, and we've got to teach our children to be different… and that comes from us as survivors. Why are we survivors ? Because we've been through it… the more impact we have, the better it is for our children. We need to teach them young.

The police, the courts, the government, and the media

needs to change because everybody's saying it's OK to be treated like this. You watch the soaps... they're getting abused, they're getting murdered, they're having all sorts of different relationships at the one time. This is what people think is normal. So what we're seeing as normal, is not normal. This is what's wrong. Children are being brought up to think everything's OK. They are being groomed, believing that it's ok to be 'liked' for their body. You see younger and younger children thinking this... and on the internet... 'sexting'.

Now it's all about media and about image... image is a massive, massive thing. Everyone who's seen on TV is skinny - usually sexy looking. What does that say about women?

Before I came to Nottingham, I came from my family home into the care system, and the same thing's happened again there. So you automatically assume, oh well that's adults - that's what adults do to children, so everything seems normalised. It's not until actually you start having your own children, and you start experiencing different feelings that you realise this is not right. There's things that you just do not understand, until you get the help you need.

People need help and they need therapy. How many people say there's bad children? It's not bad children - it's the bad upbringing, or it's the bad reception they've got from the support services who don't recognise the abuse... and so they end up not getting fixed, and carry on with the guilt, the shame, the blame... and believing it is their fault.

I know, it's hard to get out of that. Even now as a survivor at 52, I went through the same thing 4 years ago where - because I was assaulted after a relationship breakdown - I was told that I froze… and… I didn't know this at the time, because of my childhood trauma, it was an automatic response. Self survival kicking in. So he can't be charged, because I never stopped him!

So again at my age, somebody who I trusted - who I was in a relationship with for 17 years, the father of my daughter - gets away with it, and I'm the one who ends up getting a harassment charge. So I'm totally let down again.

But I'm a fighter and I will fight for justice.

I've just been to a lot of women's meetings as well, and the same thing's coming out over and over and over again. Victims of domestic abuse, whether it be sexual, financial, emotional, mental, ending up in trouble themselves - instead of their perpetrators. I went to a meeting with the Criminal Prosecution Service, and I sat next to this CPS man, who had spent 30 years as a police officer, and what was his response to me when I was telling him about my case?
        'Can't you get over it?"

Now I know why I never get justice. It beggars belief that we have these people. Why don't they get the CPS to get the survivors to come in and train them? Believe me, they need to take the time, to understand.

I'm getting people to help me, to do art and banners

for outside the courts. I want to get people who are brave enough to stand up and say, 'yes I will join you'. We will come here - like Reclaim the Night - and join you outside the courts for a day, protesting about miscarriages of justice for women.

Survivors helping survivors to me is very important because, unless you've gone through it, you don't really know. This is so important. Most places I go to now in my voluntary work, I'll say to them, 'is your worker paid or is it somebody that's a survivor?' I'd rather know now if it's somebody that's been taken in from the job centre, who's got no qualifications… or because they have been to university. The most important thing to me is whether they have experienced domestic abuse themselves or not.

Fight harder - stand up and be counted - hear your voice shout. Shout it even louder, if you have to. But don't sit back down again and let somebody put you back in that little corner. Because the more that you've shoved it back in that little corner, the more we keep it in the box and nobody wants to talk about it… 'oh, you're just being stupid.' We're not being stupid.

We want to be vocal, we want to be heard, we want justice. We want what's right. We have rights too as human beings, let alone as a woman. Don't I have the right? To not be called names? Don't I have the right to be free from violence?

We need more women judges, we need more people in the CPS that are trained in mental health and domestic abuse. They shouldn't be working without having these people in their building too. There should be no court in this land that doesn't have a domestic abuse forum inside it, or a mental health system inside it. These should come hand in hand… that everybody gets assessed, those who are vulnerable, men and women. This is what I am campaigning for.

By helping other people, going to meetings, finding out new things, attending domestic awareness courses, being in touch with other agencies, and finding out what they're doing… I'm making sure people are being held accountable. If something's not right - then speak out about it.

I work with a project which deals with abuse against children in children's homes and institutions. We're part of the Edinburgh enquiry, and also we look at the abuse that has gone on in the Catholic Church. We do a lot of networking with different organisations.

When I'm most happy is when I know that I've been successful in helping somebody else come forward to tell their story of survival, and I know I've done something that has helped that person. That's all that matters, as long as survivors can be helped. Knowing I can be part of this is all that matters to me now. People just want someone to believe and listen to them. They don't want judgement.

I still have my down days, I'm not going to lie. Most of these days happen because I'm not physically able to do things the way I used to. I do wish I had my health back, but that's another reason why I think it's important to talk about domestic abuse and emotional abuse. Because it's the impact that mental, emotional and psychological abuse can have... because it actually causes a physical impact on your body.

So if we look at records now, and we collect information from the survivors we work with... and we're noticing a pattern between the psychological and mental health and their physical ailments - they're all connected. Every single one of us survivors in my group all suffer from stomach problems, feet problems, mobility issues, sleep deprivation - all the things that are identifiable, recognisable, from a mental health perspective... and this is why it's called Post Traumatic Stress Disorder. It's the physical ailments that it causes as well as the mental elements. It all has an impact.

I can see with my daughter, she's changed because she's stronger. She won't let any man take advantage of her, and she knows that she's equal now. I've always told her that, if he's not putting in then, you know, you have to step up and say something. Don't let them talk to you and put you down. So she knows that, and she's quite strong. But I just hope that I've given her the strength and the knowledge that she doesn't have to take none of it, and that she can stand up for herself and pass it on to her children, so that they know what's right and what's wrong.

I would like to start seeing them take DVA courses into schools at a younger age, and teaching them about emotional and physical wellbeing. Instead of sex education, go and teach the children how to treat each other with respect, telling them about respecting their body, respecting each other, and having a boundary of no touch, no go. Some children are thinking its acceptable and we, as adults need to change that attitude.

I've actually written a book - it's not been published yet. It's called *Getting To Know Me Through my PTSD*. It covers my journey.

Writing the book has helped with my healing process, it's helped me to also understand, that none of the abuse was my fault. It's been such an important journey because all those years of guilt, shame, blame have stopped now. And it isn't just because my Dad has died, and stuff like that. It was that journey, the process of unlocking the baggage, getting rid of it, figuring it out. Why did this happen ? It was because it could happen. Because I was there. I just happened to be available for these people. It was nothing to do with me, and that was one of the hardest things, realising it wasn't me, because you grow up believing it is you that's done it. It's you that's wrong.

There's no words that people can understand, about how it makes you feel to feel free. You've not got that sickness feeling in your stomach anymore. You've not got that horrible, horrible, yeugh. I'm not doing any scribbling over what I should do. All the psychological damage lifting. It's a good feeling.

You actually feel empowered in the end. Nobody's

going to put you back down again, I just want to keep battling on. I don't care if it takes me until I'm 95 to get justice. I'll just keep going. So it doesn't matter how many times you keep knocking me down, I'll get back up again. That's one thing I remember, to get back up and fight. You can't keep a good woman down for long… and yeah, a survivor's a survivor, and hopefully let's keep on surviving, keep helping others.

JANE
Create your lifebelt to get you back to shore

He's the first thing I do when I wake up in the morning. Got this lovely little face that says hello. Smiley little face. Getting up to make sure that he's looked after makes me feel better about myself, because when I'm getting his porridge ready, I'm getting my porridge ready. We're having breakfast together. There's something quite sociable about having a dog - you can talk to them. They don't judge you. They just lick your hand... so long as there's food at the end of it - they don't mind. It's just one of those things, there's this kind of unconditional bond that you have. He's absolutely priceless, you can't measure it but it's there. He keeps me going. He makes me laugh and I'm sure one day he'll make me cry, but it's just one of those things - it's just magical. Even my support worker from Women's Aid when she came to visit me when I moved in, she said you're completely different, you've just gone up about three notches. Everything's more positive, you're not referring to black darkness, your negative stuff from the past. You've got a future. You've got something young that needs you, and that's it - you're really fired up, you've got more energy. You've even caught the sun a bit. You're not your pale usual gothness!

But it's just nice for someone to come in and acknowledge the fact, and I thought yeah, I do actually feel a bit better. I feel a bit more positive in myself. I've got a reason to get up, I've got a reason to fight through, to remember mealtimes, remember for me - because I've got to remember mealtimes for him. So I'm looking after myself better because I've got a responsibility to him to look after myself. We look after each other.

The genuineness and the gentleness of it all - it's so subtle that - and you miss the subtle things when you're under tension all the time. You're in the trench, you got your tin hat on, you can't see a way out of it.

Jane's story

If I can help one person feel a bit more empowered, a bit more hopeful - because it's just such a hopeless place to be when you're feeling trapped and depressed and lonely, and you feel like nobody else in the universe knows what's going on, because it all happens behind closed doors.

It's subtle things like the glares, the kicks under the table and the elbow in the ribs… it's just one of those things. Those things happen when you're out and about with other people. You just get a glare off somebody and you're thinking, better watch my Ps and Qs.

When you're stuck behind four walls… I mean I was housebound by my disability, but it was worsened by my then husband's attitude. He'd lock me in and I hadn't got a key to get out, and it wouldn't have mattered anyway because I was upstairs, and I couldn't actually get downstairs. So if the place had gone up in flames, I'd have gone up with it. It was just really dangerous, but it was also that feeling of not just being cut off physically but cut off mentally… because he can't really care, if he's done that, and put me in that position. He's got to have worked out that I couldn't have got downstairs, and I couldn't have got out. But he just had to know where I was at all times.

They've got that much control, it just erodes every little bit of strength you've got, and I think you have to have a trigger somewhere, something that fires your soul. It could be kids for some women, but I don't have kids. So for me it was my dog Freya. She and I were bonded, and we could tell at a glance what each other was thinking. She kept me going through some really hard and lonely times. But, he hurt her once, and that did it for me. I was resilient enough internally to cope with what he could do, or so I thought at the time, but knowledge and wisdom only comes with time, and you work out eventually that you're actually worth more.

I think that was a lightbulb moment for me and what finally finished it all off. We knew during the last 3 months of her life that we were expecting her to pass away. We found out on a kind of MOT check up and the vet said, 'take her home, enjoy the time you have with her', and we got an extra 3 months. I knew that it was going to cost £390 to get her cremated and get her ashes back, so I put it in a savings account, saved it up over three months. The night before we were going to have her put to sleep, I checked the account, and he'd wiped it clear and spent it all on drink and drugs. So I had to go to a friend to borrow some money to have her put to sleep, but I didn't have enough to have her cremated and get the ashes back... so that just, like a bomb went off in my stomach, and I thought - that's it. You've just done something that is completely and utterly unforgivable. That was part of my bargaining with the whole letting go of the little being that had been in my life for fourteen and a quarter years, and you just think, I'm sorry you've gone one step too far. You've done that to my dog. Nobody does that, and it won't be tolerated.

It was the subtlety of that, it just made my mind up,

I just thought that's it, I can't be with this person anymore. I really can't. You know, you're resilient enough in yourself, you're used to the rhythm of what goes on. That's the weird thing, you get used to it, you adapt to it. That's something about women, we're really good at adapting, but we're also good at adapting to bad things. Because you love someone you'll tolerate all sorts of things, and because you tolerate it the first time, it gets worse, because it's like you've accepted it and ticked the box that says that's ok, and in the background it's progressing, and the more control gets taken away from you the more control you lose… and it doesn't ever come back.

Back when benefits were paid weekly - you got your book stamped and relatives could go and get it, so of course husband goes to get it, gets the cash and so I never saw that. It got spent on drink, drugs, whatever.

I've been left just over a year now, and I've had a little lightbulb moment of realising he was on self destruct, and everything around him had to be on self-destruct as well. So it's almost like a drowning man, thrashing about looking for something to grab on to, and you're in the water with them, and they're taking you down with them, and you're subsumed by this and it's like a black cloak that comes over you, like in the Dracula films, when the whole atmosphere changes and it's almost like static, and you can feel the change. And if you ever feel that in an argument, if the hairs on your neck stand up or you get goosebumps and a twist in your gut… follow it… trust it… it will only get worse. Listen to your family, and when you introduce a new partner to them, have one of those quiet face to face conversations with each member of your family, and say what do you think of him? Be honest and if you don't like him, if you think he's a real 'you know what' you tell me. I won't be offended. Put your feelings in your pocket for a while, and let somebody else have their view. Because if my Dad had said what he was thinking on my wedding day, I wouldn't have married him… and if my brother had said what he was thinking on my wedding day, I wouldn't have married him. So if either or both of them had said I don't trust him, there's something about him that rubs me up the wrong way… something's going to go wrong. It's just a gut feeling. Trust your and their gut feelings. You don't have to tell the person you're with that you've had that discussion. You don't have to confront anybody. I wouldn't advise anyone to confront someone. But keep that in your back pocket. Notch that one up. Be a bit of an elephant. Not going to forget that one. Stick a little pin in that day on the calendar. You don't have to write anything down. Dad told me that - just in the calendar. A little pinhole. Nobody will know it's there, unless they really look for it. You've not had to write anything down that can be found, because that's one of the main things when you're trying to leave.

Once you've had the bomb that goes off in your stomach and you think I've got to go, you're thinking, how am I going to do it ? I'm in a wheelchair. I'm housebound. I've got no income apart from my benefits so I needed help. My family are hundreds and hundreds of miles away. But I couldn't get in touch with them anyway because of the way he had cut me off from everyone, and alienated all the friends that would have been able to help, so I felt stuck. Marooned.

It's almost like Maslow's hierarchy of needs. I remember, getting a book out of the library and I found this book and it fell open at this pyramid and I thought wow, if that's not trying to tell you something duck, you really are a bit thick, so I thought wow, ok, so you work from the bottom up. You've got all this, you've got all this, you've got all this now. What do you really need ? And the safety and security thing - you can't have anything safe and secure without building on that from the start. I'm not very religious, but the biblical thing of you can't build things on sand. You know, it's been written by people hundreds of thousands of years ago but you know, people have been going through these things silently behind closed doors for thousands and thousands of years,

There was an interesting time when he was taken to hospital with a quite serious neck injury, which meant he was going to be in hospital for six weeks, and I thought that'd be a brilliant time to escape… but then I thought how do I get downstairs? I don't have a key to open the door. So I had to get in touch with his friend from work. I said have you got any spare keys from his desk from work, and he said yeah yeah I can get them, and he came round, so I had a key then. Brilliant… and so I managed with his help to get downstairs, which was really difficult because I was just in my underwear and my t shirt. I got to the stage where I was downstairs and dressed and with his friend and I thought well I can't actually say anything to his friend to get any further help because he's his friend and that really cut my wings off. You need to be able to trust someone enough to say here's my passport, my birth certificate, my NHS medical card, my national insurance card. Can you keep them, and this money, in an envelope, until I need it because one day I will. If you can leave that safely and securely with somebody you can trust, who won't blurt it out by accident, if they bump into him in Tesco's... that's what you need.

It's like playing ten games of chess in the background, quietly, while not making the person who's angry with you for breathing aware of what's going on in the background. And I would have been lost without texts from my Mum. She was so worried about me, but my Mum's heading to eighty - her health's not brilliant. She felt powerless to help, and I was powerless to do anything for quite some time. I'd wanted to go for quite a long time, but while he was in hospital I started finding loads of credit card statements locked away by Mr Secret and his keys. He had even remortgaged the house without my permission!

So I'm not only being painted into a corner by the domestic violence, the manipulation, the coercion and the mishandling, but the fact that my main carer's my husband and he couldn't care less.

So the person who is in control of everything, actually is in control of nothing. It's like a train freewheeling downhill with no brakes. You're sat there thinking... it's not quite panic it's just a shaky feeling that you get in your guts, that everything's suddenly shifted.

It's dangerous. It's dangerous. It's unsafe. Everything about it.

So when I left I only had what I was sat down in, not a penny to my name. Overdrawn. But wow, feel safe - wonderful.

It was all very, very rushed and they were adapting the house around me for the first six weeks… but having my power back and spending my own money on my own things was wow - got my money - he's not nicked it. Such an odd feeling being in control of your own destiny.

I left adopting my dog until I'd got myself settled. Got dog now - we can face the world.

You've got these things that tie you to a person, tie you down with people. These little furry things you're responsible for. They didn't ask to be there. You have to make sure they're safe in this transition. Dogs and kids don't know why you've suddenly moved out.

There's so much entrapment, but it can be done. Thousands of women have already done it. Somebody else who's as disabled as me. As trapped as I was… if I can do it, it's possible for them too… and if there was just one message I can get to everybody, it's that there is always hope - you're not on your own. You may feel isolated but you can get out, and you'll know when you're ready. Women's Aid they let me do it at my own pace. They didn't say you've told us now, so you have to go to the police.

There's ways to deal with things and approach things, and it's so much calmer and less tense. Things can be solved, you just have to keep at them in the background. Like a dripping tap can create waterfalls… this water can erode solid stone, just dripping, dripping in the background - it all adds up.

It's like you've got this very tentative little golden strand - thinner than a human hair - that is holding your sanity, your hope for the future and your safety and your life.

I've been on two NG:She courses, the one for coping with stress, I really needed that - it's helped me no end. The Domestic Violence one… wow - I've learned things on that… even the awfully terribly understated way the crimes are recorded - maximum of five against one victim per year. That's awful. If you've hit a woman 23 times in a year, it should be logged as 23 times in a year and that will attract 23 times as much funding rather than five times as much - which is abysmal. Especially in this time of cutbacks, it's just cruel.

What's also so difficult about domestic violence in particular, is that it's so hidden. Always behind closed doors. Always within the bounds of that relationship. It becomes smaller and smaller and smaller and more claustrophobic, and it becomes less noticeable to the outside world, day after day after day, because it becomes more internal, and more trapped, and more concentrated - more toxic - it makes you ill. It makes you physically ill.

I want to pass on what I know to other people. With NG:She I can, as the last two courses that I've done have been so empowering. The first course - we kept in touch. There are people I'm still in touch with from that who I'll keep in touch with forever, and that's priceless in itself because when you've had all your friends and relatives cut away, you actually need to start building new friends and new relationships. I'm talking friendships not relationships. Heavy stuff… leave that for a while. Heal. Learn how you feel in yourself, and then you'll probably make better decisions - be able to twig earlier on if something's not quite right.

Some people fill the void inside them, the one abuse can leave you with, with drink and drugs. I'm filling this void with education… it feels fed, it feels satiated rather than something niggling, something empty.

When I did the first course, I spoke more in those few hours with people there, than I had to anyone in the last year. So you actually realise how isolating the situation had become. In one course to speak to people more than you'd done in a year. In two courses speak more than you'd done in two years, and so it's like in the next course I'll have spoken more than I have in three years, because it's been decades.

It's like wow, it's so empowering. You know like when you go on the coast and you open a window and you get that fresh gust of salty, cool air and it's like ooh blooming heck, that's gorgeous - it smells so sweet and fresh, and it's like you've just blown all the cobwebs away, and you didn't even realise you had lots of cobwebs. Something's cleared, something's moved. And it's really important because you sit there, you enjoy the smell of that fresh air because you've created that space for yourself... not just in your head, and in your heart, but you've actually physically done it... and to come on the other side of that. It's empowering, but again it's something you're not used to, so you have to get used to the feeling of being in power and control. It's very different.

But if you can sit back and say wow I've done it... if somebody else is in the mire, really in the trench, really going through it... if they can just hear somebody who has come out the other side saying there is hope out there, so just hang on. Just do what you need to do to survive day to day, but in the background just be pedalling or dripping, do something to create your lifebelt to get you back to shore because you've been isolated. You're on a little island, trapped inside, cut off from everything. You need to build a lifeline back to reality, back to the rest of society.

Don't go onto social media, don't go onto social networks for advice. Although some people will give you some wise advice, there are a lot of idiots out there... but get somebody who knows what they're doing, who are safe. Women's Aid are safe. NG:She are safe, and the information that you divulge won't go any further if you don't want it to. I said that at the start... the session I had at Citizens Advice, he said yep, fair enough, put his pen down and he listened and the doctor did the same. She said I'm not going to jump about reporting it. You do everything at your own pace.

That's the thing that you're worried about, losing even more control. Stick with the people who know how to speak your language, because then you've got clarity, you've got sense, you can find a level where you've got somewhere to send your paperwork safely, you've got someone to look after your documents safely. You're actually creating a bridge to your future… and you do have a future.

It's so hard to make that jump, but it's worth every sleepless night, it's worth every nagging doubt, and it's worth all the upheaval - it's worth it in the end, because you have your life back, you are you, and you are in control of your destiny for a change. It's an alien feeling at first until you get used to it. You go back a life stage, I just realised. Back before I met my partner, I was in a rented bungalow and I had a greyhound. I've reverted to how I was before I got married. I've come full circle. I've got goosebumps, as that is weird. OMG I was in a bungalow living on my own. I'd got a job. I was fit I was healthy and I'd got a greyhound.

LISA
I want to raise children who don't have to recover from their childhood

My name is Lisa Davis and I am a mother of two phenomenal children, my biggest and greatest achievement to date!

I lived in a home full of violence and cruelty, my dad was not a good man it was as if he wanted to win at everything and control every aspect of our lives. It had a huge effect on us as children and later as adults. When I was seven years old, I saw something that no child should see. Even though I try not to let it infringe on my everyday life. It is like skimming pebbles in a pond the ripples disappear but the stone's still in the pond.

For as long as I can remember, I wanted to have a family to replace the one taken from me. I met my soon to be husband and tried for 10 years to have children. Eventually I had a daughter with the help of fertility treatment. Things carried on, and four years later I had fertility treatment again, which resulted in me having a son.

I was always conscious of my kids having the best life possible. I went to college. How could I expect them to do well when I spent my days wandering the streets because I could not stand the loneliness of being home alone? I went back to get the qualifications I needed to do what I wanted to do. As a result, I was awarded an outstanding individual learning award by NCN College, followed by a City Council GEM award then an Evening Post hero's award for my work in schools with children.

I went on to be a learning champion and to do talks to audiences for Nottingham citizens. I also started a Facebook page called "Shelly's Secret" which gives out numbers for DV helplines, and helps deliver clothes and things on a small scale.

Since having my kids I think I've made positive steps to a decent life. The turmoil of all the past occasionally throws some dark days. I have come to realise though, even the darkest night starts with the brightest mornings.

It's easier to build children than it is to repair broken adults. Raise children who do not have to recover from their childhood.

Lisa's story

So I've just come out of a teachers assistant job. I was there for six months and absolutely loved it. But I'm working at the Library now and enjoying it equally as much. I've got two children - Stevie who is 17, and a little boy Ty-jay who is 13... and I love them to bits. I'm a people assistant so I help people with their enquiries... how to use the computers... do a few tutorials with them - older people - help them to use the tabs and stuff. It's a really good job - I really enjoy it. I'm a people person so I like the interaction with the children and adults. I love it.

When I was seven there was quite a lot of abuse at home, with my parents. My mum and dad were quite volatile, quite a bit of violence, and with us children as well, me and my brother and my sister... and that escalated one evening to quite a tragic event. We'd been out on a rare occasion with our dad, he didn't take us out very often. My mum had asked us to go back at a certain time, and he kind of ignored her. I think he knew he'd upset her. We kept saying, 'it's time to go home,' but he said, 'just have another drink or watch this for 10 minutes'. It was an excuse every time we said it's time to go home. When we eventually got home my mum was asleep on the settee.

When we woke her up she weren't impressed that we'd got home as late as we had. Back in the day it was half day shopping, so if the shop was closed on a Saturday, that was it, you weren't getting a dinner on the Sunday. It were closed, so she was a bit angry to say the least.

She'd said she wanted us back at a certain time, and he'd basically ignored her. So it kind of escalated quite quickly. My Mum had asked if I wanted to go to the shop with her, but my Dad was behind her and he was saying, 'say no, say no,' and because we was quite fearful of my Dad, I'd said, 'no'. But it was kind of like I was frightened… I was laughing a little bit… like a nervous laugh… and my Mum knew straight away, like - you've told her to say that - so you know, it escalated into a massive row.

It got worse and worse, and as I went into the kitchen to see what was happening my brother and sister stayed in the living room. I went into the kitchen - we have storm doors at the back door - she was trying to get out there, and he was dragging her back by her hair. My mum had seen me there and she said, 'go and get some help… go and get auntie Gladys,' who lived next door, but as I turned round to go and get help, I couldn't reach the Yale lock, I was too small. When I turned back, he was on top of her with a knife out of the drawer and he'd stabbed her. I think in the coroner's report it said 17 times… and basically that was it.

When we woke up the next day, we was just sat down in the living room with him. He was really agitated you know… reading stuff to us, and then there was a knock at the door. It was my grandad. My mum should have met her sister - my auntie - that night, and she never turned up so they was worried. We'd dragged my grandad upstairs… we'd had to open the door because he was persistent, he wouldn't go away. We'd had to open the door, and we dragged him upstairs and then that was it. My Dad ran up after him… and he (my Dad) committed suicide.

Domestic violence is not just seeing what you see, it is the conflicting feelings you have. My Dad robbed me of a real family - a mum I could have spoken to about my fertility problems, and in the end, a Dad who should have looked out for me, protected me from these men and the relationships I had. In addition, the guilt I felt of not being able to reach the door for help… let us just say I really struggled with that for a long time. Our home was not a happy home, I do not remember any happy or good memories, and as long as I live I'll never forget being woken in the night because we were leaving again… running after my Mum's angry strides as she pushed my sister's buggy, the smell of her long leather coat flapping behind her, hanging in the air.

None of us got any help like, counselling wise - it was just brushed under the carpet. I think because nobody spoke about it, I think me and my brother and sister didn't speak about it either. It was really hard. Not until later on, until we'd grown up and left home, did we really start to speak about things.

As a child growing up, all I wanted to do was get out of that house. It was like, I just wanted to have my own children and my own family, and at the same time, I was quite wary of men and what relationships should be. I fell into that pattern - misunderstanding what love was, because you was so desperate for it, if you know what I mean.

We weren't as kids, I think... well I know for a fact, if my sister was here, she'd tell you exactly the same thing... we weren't told that we was loved... we weren't kissed. You know like you kiss your kids goodnight, or in a morning, oh give us a kiss, and you know, set them off to school. There was none of that... and I think that made relationships hard, 'cause it was kind of alien.

I'm not very - y'know relationship-wise like 'I love you' 'I love you'. It's not like that, but I am aware of how that made me feel, so with my children I tell them all the time, and I kiss them all the time, and I cuddle them all the time, because I would hate them to feel about me the way that I felt about my Grandma. So I do my best to make sure they know how much they're loved, and kissed and cuddled and stuff like that.

We still walk through town holding hands and I think that sometimes people look at you a bit like - aren't they a bit old? - but I think, they're my babies, they'll never be too old.

I always wanted children. I remember a teacher asking at school what you wanted to do when you grow up, and I said I wanted to be a Mum, because that's all I ever wanted to do was to have my own family and have my own children. I tried a long time - it took 10 years - I had fertility treatment.

For the first 10 years of our relationship, it was quite volatile, because he just weren't a very nice man when he'd had a drink. Like I say, we'd been trying for kids for a long time and that probably was me being a little bit selfish, because to be fair I wouldn't have wanted my children in that kind of environment, 'cause it was just what I had. But, it weren't until my little lad were about 4, 3 or 4, when an incident happened and we'd had a bit of an argument at Christmas, and my little boy mentioned it… and I realised then that they was in a similar environment to what I was, so, we split up.

When Ty said that - when this incident happened - that's when I realised that they were seeing exactly the same thing that I was seeing. I didn't want my daughter to think it was alright to be treated like that. I didn't want her to think that's what relationships were. I didn't want my son to think that's how you treated women. I thought if they carry on seeing that, they're going to get accustomed to that, and they're gonna think that's what positive relationships are, and it's not.

So as much as I loved my partner, and I did... since we've split up he's been a massive, positive, excellent role model to my children. I think we both realised that that was the best thing we could have done for our children.

Stevie's very opinionated - she's got opinions that she thinks are right, and she sticks by those opinions. She won't abide any nonsense, which I'm quite pleased about. My little boy's really respectful - nice kid. Never been in any bother at school. He's got a knack of whoever he hangs around with at school, whoever his mates are, he knows what's right and what's wrong, and he can make the decision either to follow suit or stand back and do the right thing. In almost every single one of his school reports, it's always said that regardless of whoever he's with, whether it be the Jack the lad in the class or the knuckle down and really work hard, whoever it is, he knows not to get involved in the bad stuff or the naughty stuff, he makes the right decisions, when it really counts.

I think that's because how much of a positive influence me and their Dad have had on them, but if they'd have carried on seeing us arguing, I hate to think what their thinking pattern would have been now.

My childhood - there wasn't much love in there, so if I took the kids up or if I sent the kids to bed, I'd say I'll come up and I'll kiss you goodnight. If I was carrying on with my housework or studying - because I dIdn't start till later on - I'd go up and sometimes they'd be asleep, and they'd say to me, 'you never kissed me goodnight.' I'd say I have I have… so what I'd do is, I'd put lipstick on before I kissed them, then when they woke up in the morning they'd have a lipstick mark, and they'd say 'I've got a lipstick mark!', and I'd say that's where I kissed you goodnight last night, but you was asleep. So now they know… and now there's phones so I started taking photos when I did it, to show them.

I didn't want them to feel for any moment of time, not for a second, the way that I ever felt, because I knew growing up that it was wrong, that it wasn't a nice feeling, and I knew I didn't want my children to feel the same way.

I don't know why it took me so long to make that break

from their Dad, but I do know it's not caused them any damage, so I'm thankful for that at least. I think the children made my decision for me. I think you don't quite realise how resilient children are I think, if you've damaged them… but I don't think that there's anything that can't be mended if you try hard enough. I think if you get the children the help that they need, I don't think they're broken. They're mendable.

I've got no feelings or nice memories of my Dad whatsoever, and I didn't want my children to feel the same way, because sometimes I'd think to myself, my Dad should've looked after me - I should've had that… and that angers me sometimes more than anything else - just having them positive relationships with people that he stopped me from having.

My kids are my absolute world, and they're doing exceptionally well. My little boy he goes to the university, 'cause he's on the gifted and talented list, and my daughter, she's doing A levels and stuff. What shines through about her… both of them… is their hearts. They've got huge, massive hearts - such good kids. I couldn't be any more proud of them, even if I tried.

I don't like to big myself up but I do think we've done a good job bringing them up, and hopefully that'll carry on in the way they bring their children up and it'll carry on. If I'd failed that, I think that would've been worse than anything that you've seen. When you start doing that, they're winning aren't they?

MICHAELA – The Plentiful Poet.
It has to change something has to be done. The way we get tret when we ain't done nothing wrong

The following poems to be read ALOUD!

Michaela's story

Surviving

Fuck I slipped back again,
But he's not holding me by the throat this time

I've pulled away so many times

I look at his face all I feel is
Disgraced
And Hate
I wanna sprint but I'm stuck in his pace
The taste

of vomit in my mouth
When he touches my face

How can I hate so much
No love, broken trust
He took me away from me
The purest of my heart and anatomy
He's ruined the sound of my songs
I have to turn them off when they come on

He makes my spine
Shrivel up
I'm like a court fine
To this lust

I can't divide from his black hole
Sounds of an empty soul
He has nothing

At least when I die
Everyone will remember something
My smile my heart
The laughter at the start
Funny movement I'm so silly
Turned me from a lily

To a black rose
Put me in a glass box
And send me back home
Beauty and the beast
But you never got nicer
More fear for me I'm a lifer

Might as well stick some thorns in my chest
When you take the last hit

I must deserve it
Cause that's all you be repeating
It's my fault it's my fault
But I'm the one bleeding
I'm receding
My bones aren't healing
Take me away so fast in the dark
Running through a park
But I wake up
And remembers it's a happy dream that turned bad
Open my eyes
He's sat next to me with a fag
Blowing in my face like I'm some dirt bag

He said I was his wife and loved me
Why am I sitting on a mattress

Gained fatness
Sleep flatness
Disastrous
I was a blank canvas
He's chucked red all over me
Battle of blackness
Tactic less
Sadness
Here all over again to his badness

Might as well say bye
Cause I'm not getting out no matter how hard I cry
One day I can walk free
And he won't be able to come near me
I'm praying that I get stronger
Because I'm going to need It tomorrow

Survivors

Every time I tried to warn her about this guy
She assumed I was jus tryna take away her smile

It turns them against you
They think ur bring bad voo doo
For her and her new boo

But I jus tryna to show what she couldn't see
The badness behind his eyes
But she couldn't open hers to see

But you're my best friend and I'll have you till the end
But please take a step back and remind yourself of the fact
That all these arguments and paranoids
Don't jus come up from the soil

It swirls and twirls
Gets into your heart your mind and your blood
before you know it your heart's not pumping that love

They say we all have guardian angels
But really it's the siblings with the labels
Friends at dinner tables
Please jus take that step back and be able
Turn around and look at your angels
Your brothers
Your mothers
Your friends, they love us
Your grands and your fathers
All of your sisters,

Don't go back to that mister

It's you that makes me mad it's you
But it's not you
It ain't just a flu
That bruise isn't new

But she says

Shhhhhh stop. He's my boo.

Some man's minds aren't trained enough to see past
the thing they call sight

That why they drains women by their light
No fight
Despite

Being grown
by strong women
All in the boat
and disowned
By the thing we call home

He strict his sword
We ain't gonna see her no more
I was never against you
Just wanted you to be your self
Because was taken by this ghost
I hope
You'll get stronger and wiser
I want you to be able to shout from the roof tops
I am a survivor

She is a survivor
You are a survivor
We are survivors

15 Years

Me and my girls all together have wasted
15 years on these devil men
That pretend
That they'll never hurt us
Whirling and spinning
Broken hearts bruises and broke trust
Where's the way out
Please someone tell me now
So me and friends and live another life
It sends
Me mad
I'm angry my bones are boiling
From the devils soiling
Destroying
Removing our pure hearts
I'm fucked up I'm angry
I'm screaming for our women's hearts
Show me the fucking way out
Show me fucking happiness
Where is it?
Why does the lord from above want to send us this
destroying unhappiest
I'm done I'm not bein nice no more
Any man that comes near me I wanna destroy
I make a man hurt like he's hurt my women
Lies and lies hits and fights
Every man we been with are from
a different background
Rich ones broke ones
Smart ones low ones
They all hit us like we're no ones

No man can be different
Why the fuck are all the women's from different
backgrounds in the same predicament
I'm done I wanna kill
I just hope my son
Don't tune out like these lies of life
we been tryna dig out
I jus want some sunshine
Not no rain
Streets of light
In this painful life
So we smile and hold hands
Run through field
Like the films

Safe

Past and present no future
I just wished my mother
Hugged me more
And held me down to the floor
Cause I been floating for some while now
I got let off the leash to destroy my own self how
I used to do whatever I wanted
With whoever I wanted to do it with
Now that haunts my heart when I look at my kid and I
just wished I grown into a different type of woman
Out on the streets moving BADISH
There was no doubt I was gonna get a habit
Clear as day
I only see grey
The morning is the handleable
The night is terrible
I could sleep for a week
Give me any type of sheet
A pillow
And I'll drift to a mind that I don't require
Think about my father
How he wasn't there
To wipe my tears
Just a phone call

Always thought he was so tall
Like he reached the sky
And he's got beautiful eyesight
But
it's just another sad story
About a daughter and her sad glory

Another broken girl
In a world
To be targeted by these men
That pretend
They'll hold your heart
But treat you like some tart
Here we go again
At the start

Don't learn from your mistakes
Here again wid these fakes
A boyfriend a snake
All they do is take
And hate
Destroy
What do we live for
Broken records
Smashed doors
Broken hearts
Cries
Hopefully this person inside me dies
Start fresh
And test
Myself to live on another level
Instead of walking with the devil
Disguised
His eyes
Thought they was loveable
My heart now untouchable
Just wanna be in a place
That I'm safe.
Shut my eyes
And see pretty butterflies

Not scary dreams
With a man always beating on me

Take a breath and see
Where this road takes me
Somewhere new
Where the grass is green and the sky's blue
Normal little life on a hill
Far away from this evil

Raw

The thoughts you get in my mind when when you're
thinking about it
That force that you get when you dream about it
The magical movements you feel it in your bones
The sounds of the crowds in the lonely homes
It's a positive feeling and we ain't been feelin good all
week
Take that chance and dance till your head is weak
Then it's the cycle...
You hate it it tears you apart but still love it from afar
The further way the better,
Enforces your mind to write a letter, about the better
life you can have it, but you forget it

That letter got dashed at the back of your trash
And then you're at the start in a bar looking for faces
you can party with.
Talking about the people that you live for
How you'll cry and die and take a life for
Then the clocks ticking and you're running out of
words to say
So you speak about a life that you'll have one day
The dreams turn into nightmares
Cause the clock running out yeah
Tick e tee tock!
Then laying in a bed all alone hearing the sound of
your own foes
Wait... can you hear that? Can you see that?
Oh that's effect of the marijuana
Fuck it's meant to make me relax
Not think much harder

Gonna have to scream at the dealer
Take a couple pills to make my eyes all sleepy
Maybe one day I'll drop to sleep like a baby
Everything wears off, the songs the laughter, the wrath
of desire
And you fall asleep into a mind that you don't require
Then it's the end of the chapter
Make a new one the week after
Maybe be a different character
The party ain't gonna marry ya
But you're happy for now
In the moment
Till someone tries to make an argument
Then there's blood and tears
Don't know how we all got here
But we ain't leaving not for a while
Kiss make up and fake a smile
But we're dying inside the devil needs to get out
Before he takes your last breath there's no doubt
That your lives falling apart
But you can't leave the bar
It's not closing for another hour
And you have to people make people laugh just a little
longer
You ain't got shit to do tomorrow
So we stay up
Leaving the gutter with our heads in the ground don't
look up
Pass me them shades don't look at me, you don't speak
to anyone for a week...
When you're finally heal you're ready for another go
Just another weekend with them foes

Resilient

I'm jus growing away from everyone
I'm seeing things for what they really are it's been so long
Sitting and draining the smile from your eyes
Because you sad about a guy
And you learn from your mistake for once
Now you look around and your girls are in the same hunch
I'm trying to speak for my heart and listen too
But everyone so blinded from this life my voice ain't breaking through
I don't know what to do
Not long ago I was in the same sitch
Hit by a prick
Mind in a ditch
Now my girls are being label the devil's bitch
It's not okay it's not right
Especially when this fire warms in my heart at night
I don't feel so cold
But everyone gone to mould
I didn't recognise
Because My skies
So dark in the night
No stars in My life
Everyone's mind's gone with no dismissal
Dipped and been drowning by the despicable
How can us women be happy strong n stabs together
All my girls been taken by his stormy weather
I've got one friend that's left the country
Gave herself the new name .. misery
It's fuckery

Zoey wasted her best years on a man that
Didn't respect his women
Now she's sinking alone in the current
Another one of my ladies is dancing with the devil
He's moved her morals to a different level
Now I'm standing here finally a survivor
Trying so hard not to call my supplier
How can I guide my friends to aim higher

I'm drowning without water to speak what's on my
heart
I'm finding it hard
Disorder
Love
Laughter
Smiles today
Cries tomorrow
How can I finally be happy
Without all of my family
Was surviving the best thing to do
Cause now I'm alone
Tryna succeed on my own
Only girl that makes me laugh so hard
It's lost in the dark
The others not even in my distance
I hope she's resilient
Zoey always has been
Praying she stops having bad dreams
I'll put my hands together and pray for my ladies
So just listen,
Tomorrow can always be better than yesterday

Black Blood

Black blood running through his veins to his heart
Venom, emotional hatred the dark
I don't know why I did this to my heart

Should of known better
By the dim letter
Saying he loved me and he has me
But all letters was spelt wrong
No capital letters
And I'm the type of girl that likes to write better

I swallowed my pride the time was ticking out
Like a bird in the deep sky
Tryna fly
with no wings
cause
The wind
Rippin me apart
Tearing me limb by limb
Putting bruises on my heart

At the start

Here we go again

Trying so hard to find it in my heart
To forget all the pain

But nothing ever changed the next days was the same
The huffs and the sigh slamming from door to door
Leaving bruises all on my walls

They see everything
But they keep quiet cause they want everybody to love
him like you do
But your family seen through his voo doo

But you're blind to it
It's called domestic violence, we're deaf to the sound
of it

The passion came from the way he hit the walls
Making you feel so small
In this big world

accent american
   Shut up hater he loves me I know he does
   He only acts like this because I show him up

If you can give it u can get it even harder
Hand on my heart I blame my father
I don't want this shit all over again
these men following me to the end
I end up nothing but my fucking friends

It has to change something has to be done
The way we get tret when we ain't done nothing wrong
There got to be something
Some light some love some godly something
Cause we need it and if we don't get it I dunno what's
gonna happen trick

and when we
find it we'll love it so hard
We're beautiful creatures, delicate features, pure love

coming from our heart
We got that it's naturally inside our souls
Trying to fill these wrong holes

Our laughter comes from something so old
I just know

One day I'll get that. I have to pray for the day. I'm just
looking forward to it much more than I was yesterday

MIMI
I started to write again, and it gave me freedom

When I left the domestic violence relationship I was in, I did a lot of soul-searching and growing, and different things, and I just felt like I had to do something to help other people. I couldn't have gone through all these years of this and do nothing with it. I felt like I couldn't walk away from what I knew, and just carry on with my life. I had to use it and so I started a Facebook page, to support people who were going through it, who had left… and it did kind of work as like a little self help therapy for myself as well. I could say these things, get them out there… and so many other people were like, 'oh my god yeah! - that's how it is and that's how I feel and this is what happened to me,' and so on.

There's people on there from all over, and after looking at it and myself deeper, I thought, right there's so much out there for recovery, like… oh this has happened to you - we can help you, this has happened to you, we can help you too… but I didn't find anything that was like, hold on, this is what domestic violence is. I can tell you what it is and teach you, in a way to help prevent you perhaps from going into a relationship like that. Also, I can then tell people who I was as a person at the time, when I fell into that relationship, because as we know, these perpetrators don't come along as - 'hey,

I'm this person, and a few months along the line I might punch you in the face, and be really horrible'... they don't come up to you and punch you in the face and then you get into a relationship with them. You meet them and they are like Prince Charming.

Mimi's story

So I first got to know Ros and Jo - I came on a course to do with domestic violence, and how to help other people, and what to do… like keeping yourself safe as well, and it was really interesting and really informative… and from there I got to know women at NG:She and started doing projects of my own with them. They supported me with my poetry and other things that I do, so it was really good.

So I then developed a workshop, and took it to some youth groups, and did it with young girls. It's been on the back burner for a while, while I've been at uni, because I'm now developing it and hopefully, my plans are to roll it out nationwide, but I've got some work to do before I get there. But I just felt like, if I could say to young people, look at you, look at what society's telling you, look at all these things… and then this is domestic violence, and this is that, and you'll be able to recognise those things.

Because so many young people in relationships now don't even see that when your boyfriend or your girlfriend is saying - let me look on your phone or let me see who's texted you, that this is part of domestic abuse, control and power. It's already starting, and getting used to that is not something you should be doing. Your phone's your phone. I've got stuff on my phone, and you know, it's not that I want to hide it from people, but it's mine. Like my diary, if I were to write in my diary, what has it got to do with you? I'd had that previously in a teenage relationship and just thought it was normal, so when the bigger, badder, scarier relationship came along, there were times where… maybe I did know things were wrong, but I didn't click on to it straightaway, and by the time it was happening, I loved that person, and had no idea what the hell was going on!

I called my Facebook page 'Know Your Worth', because I realised at the time, when I was included in that, I didn't know my own worth. Now I do, and now I can recognise things. Boy, if someone was to come along, and be like him again… NO! Because I am worth so much more than that, and I would recognise it, and I'd be able to say… DO ONE!

So, being in that domestic violence relationship was intense and suffocating, and one of the lowest times of my life, even though I did have children that came out of that relationship. There were obviously points where it was happy, and I was happy with my children and stuff.

But I wasn't ever truly happy, because even those moments of giving birth and having children, were tainted by his horrible behaviours and things he would say and do… and being left alone when I wasn't actually supposed to be alone, but suffocating as well… like I couldn't be who I was, even though I didn't quite know who that was then. I couldn't be anyone. I was who he wanted me to be.

I literally did things that I never thought I'd let anyone make me do, and I changed the way I dressed, changed the nail varnish colour I wore, changed my hair, my hair colour. I literally walked around looking at the floor, because if I didn't walk around looking at the floor, I might accidentally look at another guy or make eye contact with someone.

I remember one incident… someone that I knew from school, a man, got out of his car near where I lived, and he was like "Oh hi, are you alright? " Hadn't seen each other since school, and so I was like, "Yeah, yeah, how're you doing?" And I was walking along with this person I was in a relationship with, and my child in a pushchair, but when I got home - that was it.

'Bet you wish you were with him, don't you….oh, look at him with his flash car'… and … 'you were a bit overly happy to see him'… and all of this, and I just felt like I was going insane, like, is this really happening? Are you really saying these things to me? It felt crazy, but I didn't know how to get out of it.

Even going and doing the shopping… and I didn't even live with this person. But he literally used my home like a hotel, never contributed anything, never contributed towards his children. So I'd be out at the shops, with my children in tow, and if I didn't answer my phone the first time he rang - I must be speaking to some guy somewhere.

If I didn't get back in the space of time HE thought it should take to go and do a big shop with toddlers and babies in tow… well, according to him, I had probably slept with someone while I was out. It sounds crazy now and I can laugh at some of it and I just think - did his brain really work like this?

How would I have done those things with all these kids with me, and coming back with the whole week's shopping anyway?

But laughing aside, it was incredibly, incredibly suffocating, and I did totally lose myself within that relationship.

After quite a few years of being with this person, I got to know that this was wrong. I couldn't literally do anything… couldn't be who I wanted to be. I'd had a job but during that relationship I got made redundant and was never able to find another one, because I just got trapped into being pregnant and having babies, and I do believe it was part of his blasé, 'well whatever… if you get pregnant, you get pregnant', attitude, because he never would use contraception, and didn't care about me - so what if I got pregnant? His thought was, 'oh well just have an abortion then', and, you know, 'and you don't want to do that then? Whatever.' And so I'm trapped sat there with his kids, and what can I do?

My family moved away to another city, and I was totally alone and I started to think to myself, well you know what, I am going to go back home to this city, which I wanted to do for a long time. It was part of my plan to get away from him, because I knew he would never leave where we were.

So what helped me at first was I went along to a SureStart Centre and started doing volunteer work with them, once I'd moved to this other city, because I went and I stayed with my Mum, with the kids with a plan to get a house. Because I knew he would never come, I just had to use it as…"Yeah, you know, we'll be together - you'll come one day… da da da da da." I knew he never would, so it was like my little baby steps to get away from him.

Once I'd started doing this volunteer work, they were amazing, and they started putting me on courses for maths and English, because I'd left school without anything… and once I started doing those things, I found my freedom. I started to talk to other women, and be with other mums and see what I could do, and that I could be someone. Then to have him coming up at a weekend, and go back to being like this prisoner was really, really hard, and I was torn between these two lives.

I was pretending all the time when I was at the SureStart or wherever that my life was fine, and that everything was happy and, yeah… he would come up at a weekend, and I could see it wasn't… and it was times like that, that I started to think I'm just living a lie, this isn't my truth.

I finally got a house, but he just would not go away and kept coming, and I couldn't break away from him. Then there was a really, really violent awful incident one New Year's, and I was totally let down by the police as well with that. Although it happened out of the house and my children weren't witnesses to it, my oldest daughter knew, and she just screamed at me one day and said, "Why are you letting this happen to you? You would never let this happen to me. If you don't leave him, I'm going to go and live with my Nanny…" and this broke me.

I thought I can't let that happen, I love my kids more than anything in the world, so I rang him then and there and said, don't ever come back here. We're over and it's done, and I told her you're more important, I love you more. But then the fear set in and the stalking, and I was so frightened of what he would do that I let him back. But then the guilt of that, and looking at her every day, and all of this. So I had to put things in place to make it safer than just, 'goodbye, you can't ever come here again'. Because I had children with him as well that he would have to see, and they would have wanted to see him. They were small so they wouldn't understand.

But you know, when I finally did leave and it was finally it, and I cut off, it was the intenseness as well as the fear that I felt of what might he do. He might kill me. It was texts after texts after texts, then phone calls and anything he could use to try and get me onside. Like, I was a poet before I met him, but couldn't write throughout that relationship, because I wasn't ever in a place to… and I was so lost, and not knowing where I was, how could I write about anything?

He knew that I loved poetry, but he used that as a tactic, and wrote a poem… and said 'look I've written this poem for you,' and it was insane and so draining, and then when that didn't work, it was, 'I'll kill myself. I can't live without you,' and that was so intense, because I had to stick to my guns and say, NO, I'm not being with you. At times I said terrible things like, 'well go and do it then...' and then I thought, oh my god, what if he does and dadadada? And not because I cared or wanted to be with him, but obviously it's not a nice thing.

That time was really, really difficult and really, really lonely. So lonely because I didn't have anyone around me who understood what I was going through, and the people that were around closely, they wanted me to leave that relationship anyway, so for them it was, 'You've left, yay, it's over!' But it wasn't over. It wasn't over for me in the slightest. It wasn't over because of the stalking. It wasn't over because I had traumas from that relationship, that I had to recover from. Things that I didn't understand, it was so frightening and so lonely. I think that in the past, wanting to leave and leaving... there were so many reasons why I went back, or let him back. It's that age old saying - it's better the devil you know - and it was easier because I knew what was happening. I knew what would come. I knew what it would be... and change is one of the most frightening things in the world.

But, lack of support and not knowing things - it's really difficult when you leave. One day by chance, or by luck, when I was taking my children to school, I saw a flyer for the Freedom Programme. I had no clue what it was, what it meant. But I just saw the words domestic violence, and finally admitted to myself, that is what I had been affected by.

I took the number. Got in my car and rang this number, and went on the course. But it still took a long time to get to where I am now, and heal my life, and there are still parts of my life that aren't fully healed from it. Six, seven years down the line, they're still not. I am still working on those things.

Being hit, for me, wasn't the worst part about that relationship. It was the mental and emotional abuse, and those scars are the things that stay, and are harder to get over. That's why I had to do something with what I had been through, and why I wanted to do things with young people - to try and keep them out of going into a relationship like that, and trying to smash this thing within society that's there that tells them, you must look like this…this is how you must be… this is who you must be and, as a female, you must be passive, and get on with it, and it's OK, and men must be aggressive, and stand up for you and do this and dadadadada... and then these things get confused as, 'well if he doesn't want me to see or speak to this person, it's only because he loves me and cares...' and it's not true!

You're not only the victim of that relationship and that perpetrator, you're the victim of things in society, and you have to get over those and learn what those things are as well.

One thing that really helped to bring me back to who I was, but also helped me find who I am, and then build on that person and let that person grow, and be, was education and reading books, and finally doing something that I thought I'd never, ever be able to do… and that's going to university. That really was a massive thing for me and still is… and my poetry of course!

I started to write again, and it gave me freedom… freedom to say things that I probably would never, or could never say to someone, but poetry let me. It let me do it in a way of… that I can write this, and I can say this and no-one really knows if it actually really happened to me. It's just my poem… and that really helped me as well. Then when I started to perform poetry, and I would have women come up to me and say….'Oh I could relate to that' or 'Yeah I felt that,' that for me felt like, yeah I'm doing something with this… and even if one person was affected by it in a positive way, it was enough for me.

I'm doing youth and community work, and plan to go on and do a Masters in violence against women and children.

I think it's really difficult when someone is trapped in that kind of situation and in that relationship, because until they know what it is they are experiencing, and until they know that they are more important, they are worthy of more, they are worthy of being loved, and to love themselves, it's so difficult to even say to them that, you know, after this, it's going to be OK. Because in that moment, you think, no, it's never going to be OK… I'm never going to get out of this because at times, as terrible as it sounds, the only way I thought I'd ever be free is that if he was to die, and that would've been my only escape, that's how trapped I felt.

I think a lot of women feel like that, but one thing I would say is that when you're ready, you will do it, and you will be OK and you will be FREE and you will be able to be you, and you WILL finally be happy. I never thought I'd be happy, and right now in my life at this moment, I'm the happiest I've ever been.

Mimi's Poems

Growth

18yrs ago I'd have spat this like an mc
But that old me ain't me
Anymore
They say if you ain't losing people then you ain't growing
My blocked list states 10ft tall
17yrs ago this would have been harder
Angrier
Back when I hated the world
When I'd a licked ya for one look
A lost little girl
attracting negativity in her life
Full of insecurities
Accumulated though strife
I only had his weak ass example to look to
Partly why men took the piss ended up a kid with a kid
got took for a ride
14yrs ago I started to see but not fully realise
I could achieve all the dreams I had in my mind
Not wanting to be a statistic
Ran my own business
Kept myself to myself
Worked hard to pay the bills
But financially ill
They don't teach life skills
I learned that shit over time
Two lil girls all mine
I didn't want love
Lust

Or any other bs
I had zero trust
Fucked up on the inside
while you all thought I was fine!
Fake smile on ma face
Life a tha party each night
Joker to keep ya distant
Keep your distance
You ain't getting in side
Mistakes
Mistook
Attention for love
Silly girl
But at least I kept my legs shut
Independent as fuck
But i slipped up
As he approached me in a club
Life lessons
3 blessings
But he was narcissistic as fuck
Head butts
Ain't love
Even less trust
Hated myself
Insecure
Totally stuck
Lost who I was
Who had I become
What riled him up
Arse at my table
His pockets empty as fuck
Between me, his Mum
He had the life of luxury

I was invisible
couldn't see me bruised up?
But wait
He couldn't put out what burned inside of me
The lying bastard finally ran out of luck
Weak
Pathetic
Begging for what?
Control over me slipping away and I began to see the
other side!
A new life
A new smile
A new me
but not for a while
Took steps
Covered tracks
Constantly looking back
Stalked
Text over 200 times
24hr lies
Kept him distant
But fear invaded my mind
Crippled my existence
What the fuck?!
Binge drinking to escape my existence
While he had visitation
Lonely and lost
Back to the party girl nights
Dem friends weren't friends
They were users trust!
Only good for a night
Telling me they were happy I'd left that prison cell life
They missed me for years

Yeah right
But while I needed to recover from trauma and such
They were too busy messing up their own lives
On that long list of blocked bitches and dickeads alike.
Was on my own that I'd cry.
I'd never wish it on anyone but sometimes I dreamt
that he'd die
Lower than low
I needed to rise
Education became my escape
Love grew within pages books
I was back
I could write
Poetry again
I'd found my old friend
Paper and pen
or on my phone at night
College then uni
I couldn't believe my new life
My Binkies and me happy and full of sunshine
Fuck a man I thought
But not literally
However
I was out for mine
Took time
To know me
To get shit right
Stayed single
5yrs
Two tests
Trying to get inside
saw through the lies
The universe testing me

But I was on top
Took a flight
It was on that smiling coast
That I felt at home
Africa showed me a new light
This spirituality that had always been inside of me
Could now flow freely
And been seen from the outside
always been empathetic
Now I connect on a whole other level
Never been materialistic
But leaving there
I didn't even want what little was mine
The west is a mess
Consumed by materialism
Unreality tv
I say unreality
Cause it's all bull shit to me
Mind numbing Bollox to dumb us down
I don't care what you own, who you know, where you
been
Shove ya red bottom shoes
Where they can't be seen
Rolex
I'm far to complexed
To be dazzled by your luxury
that's taken lives
In the production process
I am woman
So I am a creator
So I created myself
Forever evolving
And leaving behind

That what causes stress or refuses to rise
I don't argue anymore
Not cause I don't care
I just realise
When and where to place my energy
for the best of me and mine
Sage away your bad mind
I let the words of India and Lauryn replay over and over
Finally finding peace of mind
And I was ready for love
stopped looking
an I was able to see
This king standing right in front of me
Fell fully in love
Created a life
Little Kli-Ché
till my last dying day
he'll be the love of my life
Meant to meet
Meant to be
Made me see
I'm still working on me
Internal battles
Sometimes daily
But I don't bog the relationship down
With insecurities
I hold on to the fact that I know
I am amazing
Beautiful on the out and the inside
Do you know how long that's taken me to say out loud
and mean it?!
A long ass time!
he has the best version of me so far!

For the next up date
I'm manifesting
On us
On love
On family
On trust
On a forever after
On travel
On fun
Smiles
And sun
Loves more than an emotion
It's a decision
It's hard work and commitment
So I guess this is a to be continued
An a see ya
Till next time!

I Am Domestic Violence

I AM DOMESTIC VIOLENCE
You won't notice me at first and you can't pick me from the crowd but...I AM DOMESTIC VIOLENCE.

I AM DOMESTIC VIOLENCE
I'll tell you how special you are and shower you with compliments, I'll take you on dates, I'm slowly becoming besotted with you but you'll think that I'm great, I'll turn up unannounced because I miss you and you will think it's cute but... I AM DOMESTIC VIOLENCE.

I AM DOMESTIC VIOLENCE
I will alienate you from your friends but you won't see that's what I'm doing, I'll tell you that she flirted with me when you left the room or I saw her giving bitchy looks when your back was turned, you will begin to question your friends and your family I'm only be honest and loyal by telling you because I care so much but... I AM DOMESTIC VIOLENCE.

I AM DOMESTIC VIOLENCE
I'll tell you what to wear and how to have your hair, I'll do it so you think I'm complimenting you at first, "you look so classy with that French Polish on your nails not that pink paint with the diamonds."
"People associate blonde hair with slags I think you'll look so nice with it brown." You will slowly start to change yourself, you won't realise how I'm dragging you down. I do this because I love you so much but...
I AM DOMESTIC VIOLENCE.

I AM DOMESTIC VIOLENCE... I'll question you when you're late, I won't be taking you on any more dates. I'll accuse you of sleeping with him! He could be anyone even your cousin, you're becoming the version of you that I want you to be but...I AM DOMESTIC VIOLENCE.

I AM DOMESTIC VIOLENCE... you will have sex with me whenever I want you to, I own you, I'm here for you to please. We won't make love, you will be blessed with gifts from above that I'll make you abort or I'll tell you that I'll leave. You will be so messed up you'll beg me to stay but I'll ignore you for weeks. The kids that we have remember I'M their dad and no one will replace me! I'll tell you you're a crap mum you'll believe it cause you're dumb, I'll smack you in your face and bruise your body. I might even take your life away?! But I do all this because I love you, remember it's because I love you if you don't you won't want to stay, so I'll instill the fear that keeps you in place!!! I AM DOMESTIC VIOLENCE!!!!

ROSIE
I realised it had happened to other women and children too

My name is Rosie. I am a teacher, a feminist and an optimist (I find the third helps with the first two). I am also a lesbian and a domestic violence survivor.

One of the other women in the survivors group said to me today that we are 'warrior women,' and I thought, yes, that's exactly what we are. Part of the magnificent tribe of brave and wonderful warrior women survivors from across the world - standing up, being counted and sharing our stories of hope and renewal - welcome aboard!

Rosie's story

My dad was violent and abusive, and like many survivors I spent a lot of time sitting on the stairs as a child listening out for sounds of trouble. I became a specific target for him because of this, and I was always tired.

As far back as I can remember at night when she thought we were asleep, my mum would come into the bedroom I shared with my older sister and baby brother, and just stand at the window looking through the crack in the curtain. I always pretended to be asleep as I knew somehow it would upset her if she thought we could see her. I don't know whether the other two were awake or not, and the thought that we were all of us awake and pretending to be asleep, while she stood there silhouetted in the window trying to hide from my dad, breaks my heart… that we weren't able to just cuddle up and be scared together.

One night I could see my mum kind of playing with something in her cardigan pocket, and when my dad started coming up the stairs she took it out and I saw it flash and glint in the dark. That's when I realised that my lovely mum was terrified, and that she was hiding in our dark bedroom with a knife in her hand.

After this I would stay up sitting on the stairs at night until my dad had gone to bed and to sleep, and because of his violence my mum slept in an armchair for at least 5 years (probably longer) as there was nowhere else, other than with him, for her to go when all us kids were in bed. She got up everyday and made our breakfast and went to work, and no one, other than me knew that in fact she had no safe place to sleep.

Another night when I was about 11, he sealed up all of the windows and doors of our house with blankets and towels and turned on the gas. Fortunately one of my brothers smelled the gas and alerted me, and him and I went downstairs and turned it off and unsealed everything. No one ever spoke of this incident again, but my brother and I lived in fear of being killed in our sleep for the rest of our childhood.

One summer night, in the early hours of the morning actually, my dad was smashing the house up again, and my mum sent me and my 8 year old brother to get the police. It was about a 30 minute walk from our house. I always wondered why she did this - as we had a phone and could have just dialled 999. It was only as an adult that I realised that the reason was that she felt her children of 8 and 12 were safer out on the street at 3am than they were in their own home. This says it all about how frightened of him she was.

There were no refuges for women like my mum and their children then, and my way of dealing with it all was to continually run away from home, and I started hanging out with other young girls who had runaway, some of whom were being sexually exploited by older men. We all took a lot of drugs and I ended up quite ill with it all and was eventually taken into care, which was the fate of many children living with domestic violence and abuse in those days.

When I came out of care I was determined to make a go of my life and worked in a variety of jobs across London. One of these was in a petrol station filling up lorries with diesel. One day a lorry driver, who was a student on his summer break earning some extra money, saw me reading Simone de Beauvoir's 'The Second Sex', which I had got out of the library, and he gave me a leaflet about a residential college for people who had missed out on their education because of disadvantage, and I applied and got a place at a residential adult college in Oxford. I became a feminist during my time there, as the first Women's Liberation Conference happened at Ruskin College in 1970 and so there was a lot of feminist activity going on in Oxford, and opportunities to get together and talk about feminist politics were rife. I joined a consciousness raising group with some older woman activists and other students, and I realised through this that what had happened to my mum and I, had happened to loads of other women, and it had a political edge to it in so far as it was about men who had toxic attitudes towards women, and who felt entitled to dominate and control them using threats and violence to back up that control and that because we lived in a patriarchal society little was being done to deal with it.

After two years I was awarded the Oxford University Diploma in Public and Social Administration and I was offered a place at University. I moved to another city and worked with a group of other feminists to set up one of the first women's refuges in the UK. I have subsequently worked in the specialist domestic violence support services and related organisations in a variety of voluntary and paid roles for much of my adult life. I have also written and teach a Domestic Violence Helping Skills course for women who want to help others who are experiencing and escaping violent and abusive relationships. Most of the women who come on the course are survivors.

When I think back now, the one overriding memory I have about my childhood isn't the fear or the threats or even the violence itself, but the relentless crushing secrecy and the unspoken family rule that we mustn't speak of what was happening to us - even to one another! I wrote this poem 'Let's Say ....' as an ode to my younger self, and it reflects that feeling of hopelessness, and the incredulity I felt as a young person that none of the adults around me seemed to notice what was happening - even when we repeatedly fell asleep at school, seemed to not want to go home from anywhere, and frequently had our windows smashed and our doors kicked in for everyone to see.

This really affected me growing up, and when I realised in my early twenties that I was a lesbian I refused to start on that path of secrecy and lies again and, although it was hard, I came out pretty much straight away and lived an open and out lesbian life. Sadly, despite the fact that she did eventually get away from my dad and had a few years of peace and happiness with her friends in a new house, my mum had died of Hodgkins Disease by this time. It was a repressive time for lesbian and gay people, and my brothers and sisters were not very understanding of my sexuality. Our family was quite male dominated and as we were orphans at quite a young age, we just drifted apart and I haven't seen any of them for a very long time.

I have my own family now though. A fantastic partner and two amazing children. It was quite hard bringing up kids in a lesbian family, but we raised two amazing young people who are both feminists and we are hugely proud of them. I have met so many women throughout my life who have been badly let down by their families and it's important to remember that when this happens, you can choose and build your own family. I have a huge extended family now too, made up largely of other survivors and feminists and their children.

I have grown to be a happy, proud and optimistic adult, thanks largely to my mum, who despite everything taught me that education was really important and that sticking up for yourself and fighting injustice were necessary and noble things to do. She also taught me that it was ok to be angry about injustice too, and I believe my mum would have been a feminist activist herself if things had worked out differently for her.

I still know though how important it is, not least for all the children still living in fear, to never forget what living with domestic violence felt like.

As a lifelong feminist, I have worked in domestic violence and abuse work most of my adult life - in refuges, support services and as a consultant. I now train women, most of whom are survivors, to be domestic violence advocates and to work in domestic violence and abuse support services and I love it. I also teach a few other community courses to women. I still have enormous passion for what I do and I read all the time and keep up to date with information about the law, specialist support services and advances in theory and what's happening in other countries. I now have an MA in Women and Child Abuse too which I'm extremely proud of.

Rosie's poem

Let's say...

Let's call him Bill
It's not his name but that'll do
We're all askew anyway
I'd say
So yeah, let's call him Bill

Let's say we knew
We didn't but we flew
round
At the sound
Of shaking
And breaking
So, let's say we knew

Let's call it a row
I don't really know how we can
When a man
Breaks a nose
Then gives a rose
But let's call it a row

Let's say he tried
he didn't but he cried a lot
The plot
thickens
and sickens
So, let's say he tried

Let's say they heard

Even though it was the third time in all
They ignored a call
That night
To a 'fight'
But, let's say they heard

Let's call him Bill
Let's say we knew
Let's call it a row
Let's say he tried
Let's say they heard

Let's say oh dear but
He didn't
It wasn't
She lived in fear
They shouldn't
We couldn't

Let's say, no it's just no use
We can't stop domestic abuse

Or let's say nothing and in our silence
Think of ways to end this violence

CSS
**No more extremes, just balance in my life
- something I've always wished for**

It's not abuse if he doesn't hit you, is it? That's what I always thought. It took me close to a decade to realise that my marriage wasn't normal. He loved me, didn't he? He promised to love me for eternity.

I was the puppet on the string and he was the puppeteer. I did everything he wanted me to. I did everything possible to keep this man happy.

I kept his honour even when he trampled me beneath his feet with his ugly words and his horrible actions. I smiled that fake smile and defended him when anyone questioned the change in me. I was a woman too afraid to confide in anyone because she feared she was overreacting, too sensitive or imagining things - like he said.

He made me believe that there was something wrong with me. There was nothing wrong with me! At that point I wasn't strong enough to see the warped reality of what my marriage really was.

Women are not oppressed in Islam. The Quran is clear when it comes to the rights of women.

I was living a double life - one extreme to the other. To the world I was a happily married woman, but behind closed doors I was a victim. I was a victim of an abuse I didn't even understand. I was a victim of coercive control. This silent killer almost took my life. It was destroying me, mind, body and soul.

But I fought back and now almost two years later, I've rediscovered myself, my life and with it a purpose I never had before.

I am now raising awareness about coercive control and the effects it has on the mind and the body - the silent killer! And hoping to do much more to help women who have experienced domestic violence and control.

I am at this point in my life where I want to be, I have that balance that I've always wanted, I have my health back, I'm happy and content with what was, what is and what's left to come on this journey of mine.

If your relationship is making you ill, please seek help and advice - if you're constantly walking on eggshells; doubting your self-worth; questioning your ability to make decisions; scared; anxious; on edge; putting on a brave face outdoors and crying indoors; isolating yourself from others to keep your partner happy.

No matter what you do to keep him happy, it will never be enough. It's not selfish to think about your happiness and your health - it's necessary! Always remember that love doesn't isolate, shouldn't be conditional or controlled, doesn't degrade or induce fear.

CSS's Story

I saw a leaflet at the Women's Centre for a Domestic Violence Volunteer course, and because I want to help women experiencing domestic abuse, I thought it's the perfect course for me.

It was a night time course, and I'm not very good at going out in the dark, but I tried to face my fears, and I went. I met a wonderful group of women who understood and helped me overcome my fear of the dark as well. At the end of the course, we'd all walk down together, just making sure that we were all getting home safely, and it was amazing, just coming back every week and meeting those people and learning.

It's an issue for me because I made a mistake - I'll call it a mistake for now. I fell in love with the wrong person and he isolated me from my family, friends, work, everything. I think I became his property. He believed that he owned me. He controlled every little thing, and at the time, when you're with the person that you think you're in love with, you think if you do everything that he says, it will make the relationship better. You think he's going to like me better, you know, things are going to get better, or things are going to be the way they were when we first fell in love.

But it's not, and you learn about things like that at the course, about control. You should have a say in how you like your hair to be cut, or what size or type of clothes you like to wear. Now I know that no-one, whether it be a partner, or friend, family member, should have a say in what I want to wear, or what size I want to be. I think that was always very important to me because I always felt that if I changed myself he would love me more. If I wore what he wanted me to wear he'd love me more. If I wore high heels, even if I couldn't walk in them, he liked them, so I'd wear them. But now I can wear what I want to wear. What size I want to wear. If I want to go into a shop and I want to buy a size 18 because I'm comfortable in it, I can buy it, because no-one's going to say... oh you're not a size 18, you should be a size 10, or a size 12... and... if you're wearing a size 18, you're fat, or you're this or you're that.

You know, it feels really good to be able to go into a shop and not look at a size - look at something and try it on, whether it's a size 10 or a size 20, to just put it on and be happy and comfortable in it, because it's something that I've chosen, and something that I like. Those little things that everyone takes for granted. You know, it's things like that - you don't realise, and you start losing yourself, to become that person to make someone else happy.

I know I'm much older now, but when I look at myself, I'm where my life has stopped. I'm not 30 something, I'm still 22 years old, and I've gone back to that point where I want to go back to university, I want to study, I want to grow, and I want to become the person I would have become if I didn't fall in love with the wrong person.

We've learned in the course, about apologies and occasional indulgences. Now when I look back...

because since we've been separated he's returned some of my stuff - cards and things - and I read them now and I think, how could I have been so stupid? To look at that, I would think, oh you know, he knows what he's done wrong. He's said he's sorry. He knows exactly what he's done wrong. He's said he's sorry for hurting me. He won't hurt me again. He's sorry for making me cry. You know, he's apologised, so I should give him another chance... and now when I look at it I think, he knew what he was doing, because it's that cycle of abuse that we learned about.

I can laugh about it now because now I know that it wasn't love. What he felt for me wasn't love.

I know physical abuse is wrong as well but when he hit me and there were bruises, although it was very rare - the bruises go away. But with the emotional abuse and the constant put downs - always being told that you're useless, or you're worthless or... there are certain things I can't say as it would make me too emotional... but it's that that's always in the back of your mind. Every time someone says something good to you, you think he would say the opposite of that, and they're being positive, about the very thing he'd find wrong with me. They're appreciating that good thing about me, and it's really hard to get my head around it.

I doubt myself a lot and I wish and hope that one day I can believe in myself a bit more, and stop doubting or stop letting him come into my head saying, 'you can't do this or, nobody's going to listen to you' ...myths like that.

When I got to the refuge, again I saw a leaflet at the Womens' Centre for the Nottingham Recovery College. When I was with him, I went through quite a few years of depression. But again, because he was so controlling, he'd control what appointments I could attend, whether I'd need counselling or not. Everything had to be his decision. When I got to the refuge and I saw this, I didn't have the guts to call up myself and find out about it, because I didn't want somebody thinking I'm crazy. But there was another organisation which my occupational therapist referred me to. They're actually closing at the end of May, which is very sad. It's called Click Nottingham - for people with disabilities, social isolation, stuff like that.

The lady who helped me with that actually called up the college, and actually said she'd go up to the college with me, to support me... and I enrolled at the college. I went in. The courses that they have are amazing. They're all these self development courses, like Building Confidence, Anxiety Management, Mindfulness, Creativity through Recovery, Journalling for Recovery and you get three terms at the college. I'm actually on my third term, and I graduate in July. But because for the first two terms I did every single course that they had, to work on myself and for personal development - I didn't have a lot to do this term, so I've started volunteering. I got into volunteering because of the Recovery College.

The Recovery College also runs a course, in partnership with POhWER, that is called What is Self Advocacy, and at first I didn't take that course, because I thought it was something to do with law, and it wouldn't benefit me in any way. But it just so happened that on the day they had the taster session, something happened at the refuge and I was really upset, and I thought if I'm going to sit back home and be upset it's just going to get my mood down, so I'm going to go to college if they've got a space available on this course, I'm just going to go, freshen my mind. I got there and it was all about human rights, what your rights are, how to complain, how to be assertive, and things like that. At the end of it, there was a bit of time where you could ask the tutors for advice, or help or anything … and although they specialise in mental health, NHS complaints, and things like that, and mine was more to do with domestic abuse and an issue at the refuge, they actually gave me some really good advice, and a template on how to write a complaint.

So I took that away with me, and I wrote a complaint to the housing association about what had happened at the refuge that morning. I wasn't happy with how they dealt with it, so I used the template again to write a second complaint. It then went onto a Stage 2 and I got an apology, 2 or 3 formal apologies, and they changed the policy regarding the safety of the women in the refuge! That was self advocacy.

After doing that a lot of the other women at the refuge came to me. We got together because they weren't happy with the laundry equipment at the refuge so we wrote complaints. Everyone complained together, which was group advocacy, and we got the Housing Association to redecorate the laundry room. We got new washing machines and driers, so that was another success.

After that I signed up for another course which was called My Voice, My Choice, and at the end of it I asked if I could volunteer for them, and I'm now a volunteer and learning more about mental health. Before, I thought that anxiety and OCD were the worst mental health issues anyone could have. I've now learned there are so many more mental health issues that people need help with, and that there is so much that can be done for people with mental health issues. I know that a lot of women who experience emotional abuse suffer with mental health issues because of that, and it's nothing to be ashamed of, no matter what race or religion you are.

If you're suffering with something, and you need help for it, you shouldn't be judged, and you should just go out and get that help. I've had a lot of help from a lot of charities, from a lot of organisations, and my family's been amazing. I think having my family back has been the biggest blessing of my marriage ending. Yes, just having that support. Knowing that they're there for me, no matter what.

It's not easy, and I don't want to say to anyone, that you know what… your marriage ends, you go into a refuge and then after that, you know, in a week's time you're back to normal, you know, your life's how it used to be - it's not. You have to constantly work on yourself. Every day's a challenge. If you want to become who you used or a better version of what you used to be, and leave the person that you were with him behind. It's a challenge every day. To wake up and say now today, I'm going to do this. I know this scares me, or I might not be able to do it, I might fail, but I'm going to try - at least I tried and I'm not going to regret it.

I've set a lot of goals for myself, but I'm trying to be realistic. Although a lot of people encourage me, and say I'll reach those goals. I've given myself 5 years, because I think that it's realistic. I think 5 years is a good benchmark.

I'd like to think that places like this or courses like this can be available everywhere, not just Nottingham, and if it helped me as much as it has, I'm sure it can help a lot of other women, or other people with mental health issues.

I want to help other women who have been through it, and I am helping women with mental health problems now.

I was only at the refuge five months, but you know, in that time, they took the children to quite a few places and although I didn't have kids, they always let me go along because I'm a kid myself you know. They said you're going to enjoy this and the kids love you. One of my friends from the refuge had two boys and they would say, we want her to come, she can be one of our mums. It was really nice because we went to Skegness, and I've never been. With my husband, he'd want to go on the best holidays out of England, so I never got to enjoy the little places that are here to enjoy. It was really enjoyable with the women and kids from the refuge, the staff, support workers, it was a really good day out. Something I'll remember for the rest of my life.

Everyone still has that inner child, no matter how old you are, you still have that inner child in you. Now that I've left… and I know it sounds silly to some people… but, for me, if the weather's nice and I want to go to the park, and I want to go on a swing and just be free, I just go and play on the swings. I don't care if people are looking at me, but it's making me happy. I'm being mindful, I'm enjoying the breeze, i'm enjoying the view. I'm smelling the flowers, and I'm happy, so I don't really care what anyone else thinks

No battle is fought and won without support and I have many to thank. The Almighty God, my family and friends, Women's Aid, the NHS, the police, CLICK, Nottingham Recovery College, POhWER and of course NG:She and the Survivors project and all the amazing woman I've met on this journey.

CSS's poem

Behind Closed Doors

To the world you have the most handsome, caring, loving, funny, kind husband!

Behind closed doors when it's just you and him, the cruellest most insensitive person comes out from behind his mask, and mentally and emotionally drains everything from you. You lose yourself completely and become someone you think he will be happy with, but no one and nothing can make him happy because happiness isn't his true nature - misery is.

To the world, you are so lucky because he takes care of you and provides for you financially.

Behind closed doors, you're constantly being told how useless you are, that you'll never know the value of money and the hard work that goes into earning because you're lazy! You're stupid! And much more!

When you suggest working to help him out, a traditional set of rules come out:

It's the husband's duty to provide for his wife.

The women's duty is to stay at home and look after the family.

Then the aggression kicks in and the defensive questions start:

Are you short of anything?

Why do you want to work if you have everything you need?

Do you want people to talk bad about me? Is that why you want to work?

Either way, you lose, everything is always your fault

The home and mobile bills are on his name-itemised so he can see who you call and if its someone you're not allowed to speak to, be prepared for the worst!

Your family isn't allowed!

To the world, you are spoilt because your husband whisks you off on holiday to the finest 6star hotel, business class flights, designer handbags and clothes-oh, how pampered you are!

Behind closed doors, you don't have a penny in your designer purse and have to beg for the necessities because he is in charge and controls all the finances! Because he controls the finances, he also controls what you wear or if and when you need a haircut ,and everything else you should have a say on !!!

To the world, you are his beautiful wife - he occasionally jokes about your weight, height, voice and other personal attributes in front of others out of love - really?

Behind closed doors, he constantly puts you down -

you begin to feel like you're the ugliest person on earth and this leads to depression!!

To the world, you try not to meet family and friends without him because you're a good wife!

But if you do, then behind closed doors he gives you the silent treatment because you left him to fend for himself, you don't care about him, you're selfish, or want to meet them by yourself so you can talk bad about him - you eventually stop all contact and to keep him happy and try to make your marriage work

To the world you are happily married!

Behind closed doors you eventually realise something is wrong and try to leave

He stops you!

He says he's sorry and things will change! You see that glimmer of hope - the person you fell in love with is still somewhere inside him - you stay!!

But

The reality becomes clear after this you realise the person you fell in love with never existed !

His control, anger, aggressiveness, possessiveness and behaviour towards you gets worse because you tried to leave him.

He's isolated you from everyone

You have no one to talk to

Your body starts to give up on you

He gets scared and abandons you to save himself

He didn't love you, He abused you

He took away your basic human rights

Your RIGHT to work

Your RIGHT to socialise

Your RIGHT to be who you want to be

Your RIGHT to liberty and freedom

Your RIGHT to pursue happiness

Your RIGHT to make your own decisions

Your RIGHT to control what happens to your own body

Your RIGHT to be independent

TRACEY
I had to start my life as new

My life is all about me and what feels right for me at this present time. I've still got a long way to go in my recovery. I now take each day as it comes. I know one thing though. No one will ever tell me what I can or can't do with my life.

Tracey's story

I was born in Birmingham in June 1966, and I lived there for about 5 years, with my Mum and Dad… also my two sisters and a brother. My Dad was a long distance lorry driver, and mum worked part-time as a domestic. While mum worked, I was in charge of the younger ones, as dad was not around much… and when he was, he spent all his time drinking, and he had a violent temper.

We moved to Cradley Heath in the West Midlands when I was about six years of age. This was the pattern of my life for the next few years, where I looked after the younger ones, and dad hitting my mum when he had been drinking. There was normally no reason for it. It was not an enjoyable childhood for me. A lot was expected of me, even at a young age. This was how things was until I was 14 years of age when my life changed forever.

I was involved in a collision with a van. The driver didn't stop. I suffered a fractured skull and my leg was broken in 3 places. I was in plaster for 6 months. I had to learn to walk again. Then I was raped at 15 years of age. It was a traumatic time for me. I felt unloved and not wanted by anyone. I went off the rails - started taking drugs, and drinking too much alcohol, and went round with the wrong type of people. Started staying out at night. Eventually my mum had enough of me, and social services got involved. I was taken into care, and made a ward of court till I was 18 years of age.

This was a horrible experience - moving from one care home to another, and foster home to another foster home. I never felt I belonged anywhere, and I had no support or love.

When I was 17 years of age, I met this guy. I did not like him at all but he said I could stay with him. It was a way out of the care system, but he had complete control of me... and he was very violent to me. I just seemed to think it was normal, due to my past experiences. I got pregnant by him when I was 19 years of age, which made matters worse, as he did not want children at this time. I had my daughter, but I let my mum adopt her. It broke my heart doing this, but I was a complete mess at this time.

I fell pregnant again when I was 22. I gave birth to my son - I was keeping this one, no matter what anyone said. I went on to have another son and daughter. I had very little support and no money. Plus, my partner was still being abusive to me physically and mentally.

Once they all started school, I went back to work part-time, and my partner hated me working and earning my own money. His temper was getting worse, but I could not leave, as I had nowhere to go with 3 kids. I just put up with it - until one night... he went too far. I reported him to the police and he was charged with assaulting me.

I eventually forgave him, but if he was coming back home, it would be on my terms - he had to attend anger management classes; I took his name off the tenancy, and all income was in my name, so he lost all control over me, and he never hit me again, because he knew he'd lose me and the children.

Due to all the stress and worry of him, I started drinking again to block out the pain I was suffering at this time. After 2 years like this, I decided I needed to sort myself out. Left the West Midlands and moved to Nottingham. Got myself clean and started university - doing my youth studies degree, and I got a house so the kids could stay with me.

From this date on, I had a very close relationship with both my sons, as I explained everything about my life, and my reasons for leaving them behind, although my relationship with my daughter was not good, as she finds it difficult accepting my mental health issues, and alcohol issues.

Life was finally getting good for me and my children, although it was not meant to last, as I lost a very close family friend very suddenly. It affected both of my sons, and I'd lost my rock. He'd been with me through my worst times. I was gutted, so turned to the bottle for comfort, but I needed to sort my life out again.

I started therapy to deal with past issues. It was going to be a long couple of years, and it's still ongoing now. This is mainly due to working out my relationship with alcohol, and why I always go back to it when I have ebbs in my life. Plus I need to accept my past and move on, which meant I had to start my life as new. Working out which direction to go in was very difficult and very painful, but my sons have been a massive support to me, and have been there throughout my recovery, and still are now.

NG:She WHO WE ARE

NG:She is a Nottingham based feminist CIC established by Ros Forsey and Jo Welch in 2015. Our purpose is to empower women and girls by creating safe spaces within which women can talk, listen, perform and learn.

We work across the UK, but mainly in Nottinghamshire, and we seek to play a role in ending violence against women and children.

If you would like to enrol on one of our existing courses or talk to us about helping your organisation with an event, project or training course, please contact us at:

info@ngshe.co.uk

07850 524 319

Follow, like, and direct message us on Facebook here:
https://m.facebook.com/ngsheNottingham/

NG:She Company no: 956142

THANKS

Sincere thanks from Jo and Ros, founders and directors of NG:She CIC go to:

All of the women who have shared their stories in this book and in the podcasts with such bravery and candour. You are warriors one and all.

Karen Ingala Smith for supporting this project by looking at the first draft of and writing a foreword for this book, and for taking time to liaise encouragingly with us.

Nicole Westmoreland for her continual support and practical input to our Domestic Violence and Abuse Awareness and Helping Skills courses over the past year and for the quote from her brilliant book 'Violence Against Women: Criminological perspectives on men's violences.'

Anne Holloway from Big White Shed for helping us, with patience and sensitive enthusiasm, to navigate the publishing process.

Emily Catherine for her generous contribution to the cover and Rebecca Shore for proofreading.

Our host venues: Antenna Media Centre, Broadway, Sherwood Community Centre and Nottingham Writer's Studio

The National Lottery for their financial support.

HELP & SUPPORT

If you or anyone close to you is experiencing domestic violence and abuse, then please use the following guidance and helplines:

In an emergency, please call the Police on 999
For non-emergency calls to the Police, please use 101

Free 24 hour National Domestic Violence Helpline run by Women's Aid and Refuge
0808 2000 247

Free 24 hour Nottinghamshire Domestic Violence Helpline run by Women's Aid Integrated Services
0808 800 0340

FURTHER SUGGESTED READING

We use the following books, websites and publications to help us plan NG:She's Domestic Violence and Abuse Awareness and Helping Skills courses. They build on the themes in this book and may be useful for those wishing to find out more:

'Violence Against Women' by Nicole Westmarland, (2015), Routledge

'The Concept and Measurement of Violence Against Women and Men' by
Sylvia Walby, (2016), Policy Press

'Moving in the Shadows: Violence in the Lives of Minority Women and Children' by Liz Kelly, Yasmin Rehman and Hannana Siddiqui (2012) Routledge

Women's Aid website:
www.womensaid.org.uk

Refuge website:
www.refuge.org.uk

The Femicide Census - profiles of women killed by men

Femicide is generally defined as the murder of women because they are women, though some definitions include any murders of women or girls.

Femicide has been identified globally as a leading cause of premature death for women, yet there is limited research on the issue in Europe.

The latest Femicide Census report, published in December 2017, reveals that 113 women were killed by men in England, Wales and Northern Ireland in 2016. Nine in ten women killed that year were killed by someone they knew, 78 women were killed by their current or former intimate partner and 65 of those were killed in their own home or the home they shared with the perpetrator.

You can access The Femicide Census here:

www.womensaid.org.uk/what-we-do/campaigning-and-influencing/femicide census